SOCIAL SECURITY?

SOCIAL SECURITY?

WHAT'S IN IT FOR YOU

ETHAN POPE

MOODY
PUBLISHERS

CHICAGO

ISBN: 0-8024-0973-3
ISBN-13: 978-0-8024-0973-7

LIBRARY OF CONGRESS CATALOGING-IN-PUBLICATION DATA

Pope, Ethan.
    Social Security: what's in it for you / by Ethan Pope.
        p. cm.
    Includes bibliographical references.
    ISBN-13: 978-0-8024-0973-7
    1. Social security—United States. 2. Retirement income—Government
policy—United States. I. Title.
    HD7125.P66 2005
    368.4'3'00973—dc22

                                                                    2005022239

1 3 5 7 9 10 8 6 4 2
Printed in the United States of America

ACKNOWLEDGMENTS

THANK YOU . . .
to everyone at **Moody Publishers** who worked on this project. You are loved and appreciated. It's an honor to be on the same team with you. My special thanks to Greg Thornton, for your words of encouragement and commitment to the Financial Alert Series. I am blessed to have you as a friend; and to Jim Vincent, for your editing skills, probing questions, and commitment to excellence.

to **Juanita McConnell, Murrel and Martha Slaid** for spending hours reading the original manuscript and providing me with valuable initial feedback. Your enthusiasm for the project was contagious.

to **ministry partners** who are so faithful to pray for our ministry and support it financially.

to **Janet** for being my best friend. We did it again! Your corrections, suggestions, deletions and red ink pen helped to make this a better book. I am blessed to be married to someone like you.

to **Natalie and Austin** for always cheering me on. It's great being your dad.

QUICK FACTS

Social Security is the only source of income for approximately 22 percent of the elderly.

For one-third of Americans sixty-five and older, benefits make up 90 percent of their income.

About two-thirds of Social Security beneficiaries receive 50 percent or more of their income from Social Security.

More than nine out of ten individuals age sixty-five and older receive Social Security benefits.

By 2031 there will be almost twice as many older Americans as today — from 37 million today to 71 million.

Sources: www.whitehouse.gov,
www.ssa.gov/pressoffice/factsheets/basicfact-alt.htm

CONTENTS

THE ALERT

Has America lost her financial conscience?

ON AUGUST 14, 1935, President Franklin D. Roosevelt signed into law one of the most historic pieces of legislation in our nation's great history: the Social Security Act of 1935. From just over 200 thousand in 1940, the number of beneficiaries has grown to almost 50 million in 2005. Millions of American workers, spouses, and their children have benefited over the years from this momentous legislation.

How did it come about? As a nation we had moved from the prosperous and partying Roaring Twenties abruptly into the Great Depression of the thirties. Our banking system collapsed in 1933 when millions of panicked Americans rushed to their banks to withdraw all their savings.

It came at a time when more than 14 million Americans were unemployed. People were beginning to lose hope.

The American dream had turned into the American nightmare because of the stock market crash, the Great Depression, unemployment, the banking collapse, and a general sense of hopelessness.

Some children watched their parents dig in garbage cans to find scraps of food to feed their family. Homes were being foreclosed. Farms that had been in the family for years were being sold or foreclosed. And many senior citizens, who had worked hard their entire lives, lost everything and were left literally penniless. For a good idea of what life was like for many families during these years, rent the film *Cinderella Man,* the story of prizefighter Jim Braddock. The heavyweight contender fed his family watered-down milk and razor-thin deli meat and later told reporters he fought so he could buy milk for his family. It was not a proud moment in American history, but a painfully sad moment.

Courtesy of Social Security Administration

In his inauguration speech in 1933, President Roosevelt determined to renew America's hope. He proclaimed to the nation, "The only thing we have to fear is fear itself." He also pledged that no American would go hungry.

A NEW DEAL: SOCIAL SECURITY

President Franklin D. Roosevelt believed the citizens of this great nation needed a "New Deal," and he was determined to deliver. And deliver he did. The Social Security Act was just one aspect of President Roosevelt's New Deal.

On August 14, 1935, when President Roosevelt signed into law the Social Security Act, he said, "We can never ensure 100 percent of the population against 100 percent of the hazards and vicissitudes of life. But we have tried to frame a law which will give some measure of protection to the average citizen and his family against the loss of a job and against poverty-ridden old age." (His entire statement appears in appendix C.)

Courtesy of the Social Security Administration

President Roosevelt wanted to build what he called a "safety net." His goal was to ensure that every senior citizen could live above the poverty line. The initial Social Security Act paid retirement benefits to the primary worker and established a national unemployment compensation program.

ENDING POVERTY FOR THE ELDERLY

This landmark legislation helped to shape the overall economic landscape of our nation. When the Social Security Act was passed, an estimated 50 percent of senior citizens were living in poverty. The intent of Social Security was to prevent poverty at these levels from ever happening again. Now, seventy years later, that number has dropped to about 10 percent. It is estimated that **without Social Security today, once again 50 percent** of our nation's elderly **would be living in poverty.**

Many believe the Social Security Act of 1935 was the right thing to do at the time. Others argue it set our nation on a path of uncontrollable social welfare and bigger government—that we have yet to overcome.

Today one in six Americans receives a check every month from the federal government; more than forty-seven million people in 2004! That number is expected to reach almost sixty-nine million by 2020.[1] One side sees these numbers as a great American success story, while the other side sees this as a government program out of control.

As our nation has aged, so has Social Security. On August 14, 2005, Social Security celebrated its seventieth birthday. Along the way it has been revised and expanded, even adding medical coverage under the important (yet endangered) Medicare plan.[2] Just as many Americans begin to experience *challenges* in old age, we are finding that Social Security is no exception.

FINANCIAL ALERT, ALERT, ALERT

Here are six of those challenges:
- In only forty-five years (by 2050) Social Security and Medicare will consume 67 percent of the federal budget, according to Congressional Budget Office projections. The CBO projects other trust fund programs will consume 8 percent. This only leaves 25 percent of revenues available for other purposes.[3]
- As of 2005, the Social Security program has a $4 trillion gap between "funded benefits" and "promised benefits" over the next seventy-five years. That means in addition to the collected payroll taxes, our government needs to come up with $4 trillion over the next seventy-five years.[4] (This number is in 2004 dollars.)
- If we use an infinite horizon in our projections, the Social Security program has a $11.1 trillion shortfall between "funded benefits" and "promised benefits."[5]
- The federal government owes the Social Security Trust Fund $1.7 trillion dollars. This is money taken out of the trust fund and already spent on other government programs. (More on the infamous trust fund in chapter 4.)
- The problems with Social Security, Medicare, and the national debt threaten the long-term financial solvency of our nation.

- *America is losing her financial conscience.* America is quickly losing her financial alertness. America is charting a path of unsustainable spending, increasing entitlements, escalating debt, and greater-than-ever taxation.

It does not matter how much of an optimist you are; we are a nation destined for a disaster, unless we change our course—*and the sooner the better.* Some might reject my analysis, but we are approaching a point of no return, and the consequences will make the Great Depression and the more recent events of 9/11 (the 2001 terrorist attacks on New York and Washington, and on the plane that went down in Pennsylvania) pale in light of what is to come.

Unless we can begin charting a new course, our nation *as we know it* will no longer exist. Our economy will stagnate, our lifestyle will diminish, our educational system will deteriorate, and our national security will weaken.

Don't just take my word; read what David M. Walker, the comptroller general of the United States of America, is saying: "Continuing on our current unsustainable fiscal path will gradually erode, if not suddenly damage, our economy, our standard of living, and ultimately our national security."[6] Speaking before the House of Representatives' Ways and Means Committee, Walker concluded, "Failure to address the Social Security financing problem will, in combination with other entitlement spending, lead to an unsustainable burden on both the federal government and, ultimately, the economy."[7] Mr. Walker is a highly qualified financial expert who knows what he is talking about.

Yes, major problems are on the horizon. However, there are solutions to every problem our nation is facing—including Social Security, Medicare, and the national debt.

A Book to Educate and Change a Nation

When Moody Publishers asked me to write a book on Social Security, I took their assignment very seriously! I believe this book can not only help to educate a nation about Social Security, but can (1) change a nation, (2) influence individuals, and (3) financially impact generations to come.

Will you let me be your financial pastor for the next few hours? And after you finish reading this book, if these words ring true, would you help me deliver an important word to America by spreading this message of warning and of hope?

As a nation, we need to pray, call out to God, be active in our government, and take personal responsibility for the direction of our nation and *our personal lives.* As a people, we cannot always depend on our government to take care of us—nor in my opinion should we.

Social Security is not really about accounting procedures, but is about (1) addressing our fundamental values as a nation, (2) sounding an alarm, and (3) exhorting Christians to begin taking personal responsibility!

Many people are feeling somewhat *insecure* about Social Security. The world in which we live is full of *insecurity,* but from a biblical perspective, *authentic security* comes from but one source: God.

As believers, one of our God-given responsibilities is to be on the alert. Webster defines alert as: "watchful and ready, as in facing danger."[8]

This book is a specific call for Christians to be *on the alert* and will provide key facts, tables, charts,

potential solutions, and biblical perspective on the topic of Social Security.

In the following chapters I will be answering the essential questions we all need to be asking:

- Are there valid reasons we should feel insecure about Social Security?
- What am I not being told that I need to know?
- What went wrong—or did it?
- How much money actually remains in the Social Security Trust Fund?
- How can we save Social Security?
- Will private accounts help to permanently solve the problem?
- Are there any new ideas we should consider?
- What is the biblical response to Social Security?
- What should I be doing to prepare for the future?

My challenge to you is simply this. Read this book. In fact, study it. Become familiar with what is going on in our nation. Then, will you help me to get this important message out?

As Americans, we have the greatest potential of any nation in the world to use our resources for good. Christians in the United States have much potential to play a significant role in helping reach the world for Christ. However, if our nation stumbles or collapses financially, our potential to use our vast resources for good will vanish forever—a lost opportunity.

We cannot let that happen.

We must ACT NOW. The longer we delay in addressing Social Security, Medicare, deficit spending, and our growing national debt, the greater the consequences to come. By the way, as you will learn in this book, all four of these issues are intricately connected to each other.

In response to the challenging problems and *insecurity* our nation is facing, I offer you my second book in the Financial Alert Series: *Social Security?*

NOTES
. . . .

1. Government Accountability Office, "Social Security Reform: Early Action Would Be Prudent," 9 March 2005, report GAO-05-397T, 2; www.gao.gov/new.items/d05397t.pdf

2. Medicare has its own separate fund but is considered part of the Social Security plan. As such, this program is actually in more financial trouble than Social Security.

3. Congressional Budget Office, "The Impact of Trust Fund Programs on Federal Budget Surpluses and Deficits," Long-Range Fiscal Policy Brief, No. 5, 4 November 2002; www.cbo.gov ("Frequently Requested: CBO Briefs").

4. Social Security Administration, "2005 Annual Report of the Board of Trustees of the Federal Old-Age & Survivors Insurance & Disability Insurance Trust Fund," 5 April 2005, 56; www.ssa.gov/OACT/TR/TR05

5. Ibid., 58.

6. Government Accountability Office, "Social Security Reform: Early Action Would Be Prudent," 1.

7. Ibid., 5.

8. *Webster's New World Dictionary of the American Language,* 2nd college ed., s.v. "alert."

CHAPTER 1

THE INSECURITY

Should we feel insecure
about Social Security?

WHILE I WAS IN THE MIDDLE of researching and writing this book, my daughter, Natalie, came home from college for the weekend. Those of you who read the first book in the Financial Alert Series, *Cashing It In: Getting Ready for a World Without Money,* may remember that Natalie was the "first Pope" to own a debit card—a MOMENTOUS event in our family.

Sunday, after we returned home from church, finished eating lunch, and were sitting at the table and talking, she asked me about my new book on Social Security. It was very kind of her to ask about my book project, but I had no intention of taking the rest of the afternoon and boring my twenty-one-year-old daughter with all the details about Social Security.

So, with this in mind, I gave her a five-minute history lesson and commented on a few important dates.

Before I realized it, I had filled up the back of a manila file folder with notes, dates, problems, and even diagrams about how Social Security worked. Natalie was somewhat surprised at the extent of my research when I began pulling out of my research file "original" newspaper and magazine articles about Social Security that I had been saving for over seven years. I also showed her the multitude of articles that had been published in the last few months.

The more I talked and drew diagrams, the more her level of interest seemed to grow. Since one of my first attempts to explain my findings about Social Security appeared to be such a great success, I decided to use my "manila folder notes" as an outline for this chapter!

Here is basically what I told Natalie (with a few added notes). I hope you find it as fascinating and helpful as she did . . .

THE BEGINNING

Social Security began in 1935, when our nation was in a crisis. President Franklin D. Roosevelt signed into law what has become known as the Social Security Act of 1935. It has become one of the most well-known yet "technically" misunderstood programs in our nation's history.

As I diligently researched the information to write this book, I discovered several alarming or "unknown" facts about Social Security.

I remember on several occasions sitting at my desk, researching and reading about Social Security and discovering one of these "unknown facts." I would just sit at my desk and ponder. Sometimes I would ask myself in a sarcastic way, "I wonder how many people in America know about *this one?*" On other occasions I would have to get up from my desk and go drink a glass of milk and eat a few chocolate chip cookies, just to help ease the pain.

Now for a very important question. Do I believe these alarming facts were intentionally being hidden from the American people? No.

In other words, is this a government cover-up? Absolutely not.

All the research I am about to present is public information that I primarily found on government web sites. I believe the Social Security Administration (SSA) has developed one of the finest Web sites; you can find just about anything you want to know about Social Security at www.ssa.gov. The SSA should be applauded for their outstanding work.

Do most people know these "public" facts? No.

Why not? Very few people have ever summarized this information in a simple, straightforward manner. The goal in writing *Social Security?* is to take an enormous amount of information and summarize and present it in a logical, simple, and well-organized format.

Here are seven key—and alarming—facts I discovered that I believe every American needs to know.

ALARMING FACT # 1

PAY AS YOU GO

From its inception in 1935, Social Security was designed as a pay-as-you-go system.

What do I mean by that? The money being **paid in this month** by workers will be used to **pay out this month** the retirement benefits of those already retired.

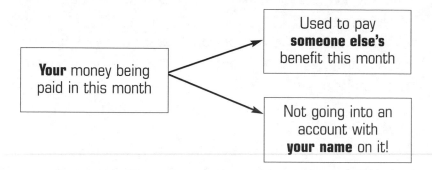

Here is the alarming fact that most people don't understand! The money you pay into Social Security today is being *spent*—not saved and put into an account "with your name on it" in order to pay your benefits in the future. The government is not taking your money and "holding it for you" until you retire.

If you are working, you are helping to pay for your parents' benefits, while your children will be helping to pay for your benefits. The younger generation has to take care of the older generation.

This pay-as-you-go system does not lean toward stability, but *instability*. In addition to projected payroll taxes to be collected, the Social Security program must come up with $10.4 trillion more over the long term in benefit money.

A pay-as-you-go system could potentially remain in balance as long as (1) you have considerably more workers than retirees, (2) people are not living longer, and (3) birth rates do not decrease. However, when these trends do not remain in place, the program's financial condition is no longer stable, but headed for insolvency —exactly where we will be in a few years.

No Legal Right to Benefits

In a recent survey that I conducted, 100 percent of the people said they felt the government had a legal obligation to pay benefits to those who have paid into the system. Unfortunately, that is simply not true. The Social Security Act of 1935 clearly states: "Congress has the right to alter, amend, or repeal any provision under this Act."

In a 1960 Supreme Court case, *Fleming v. Nestor,* the Supreme Court ruled that individuals have no legal right to demand that Social Security benefits be paid to them in the future. Of course, everyone believes the federal government will fulfill the intent, but the administrators have no legal obligation to do that! The bottom line is the United States government will fulfill this obligation out of a moral reason, not a legal reason.

Average Monthly Check

After paying payroll taxes every paycheck for forty-five working years, how much do you think the average beneficiary will receive each month from Social Security in 2005?

(a) $555 per month

(b) $955 per month

(c) $1,955 per month

(d) $3,655 per month

According to the SSA, the average 2004 monthly benefit for a retired worker is $955 per month ($11,460 per year). There is no minimum guaranteed benefit. Meanwhile, the average couple receives $1,574 in combined monthly benefits, or $18,888 annually.

When I told Natalie about the "average" benefit, do you know what her first question was? "If Bill Gates were to retire today, how much would his monthly check be?"

According to the SSA, the maximum 2004 monthly benefit being paid to *anyone* who retired at age seventy (allows maximum benefits) is $2,111. I told Natalie the maximum paid to anyone retiring at age sixty-five is $1,784 per month. The maximum paid to anyone taking early retirement at age sixty-two in 2004 was $1,422 per month.

Then Natalie asked me, "Why so little for Bill Gates?"

There are actually several reasons why, but the primary reason billionaire Bill Gates would only receive $1,784 in monthly benefits (if he retired at age sixty-five) is because the government does not tax payroll income that exceeds $90,000 (in 2005). Only earnings *up to* $90,000 are taxed for Social Security; however, there is NO CAP for Medicare payroll taxes. (More about the payroll salary cap later in the book.)

If anyone is expecting Social Security to provide the same level of lifestyle they had while working, they are going to be in for a huge surprise when they receive their first check in the mail!

I recently asked a retired person her thoughts about her *first check*. First of all, she was shocked. She said, "It's impossible for me to live on this much money each month. I am going to have to keep working." Obviously, she did not understand that the original intent of Social Security is to subsidize, not completely provide! The truth is very few Americans understand the original intent of Social Security. (See Alarming Fact #4.)

In 2000 the SSA began mailing out Personalized Earnings and Benefit Estimate Statements to everyone a few weeks before their birthday. This mailing hopefully has helped citizens have a realistic expectation as to the projected benefits they will be receiving at retirement.

SOCIAL SECURITY
FLASHBACK

When Social Security began, the maximum payment a qualified worker would receive was $85 per month, and the minimum amount was $10 per month. (www.ssa.gov/history)

ALARMING FACT #4

Number Who Depend 100 Percent on SS

The SSA has documented on its Web site that 22 percent of Americans over the age of sixty-five depend on Social

Security benefits for all their income.[1] Now, that is a lot of people.

Therefore, if for some reason the Social Security system could not send out benefit checks, 22 percent of our senior citizens would have ZERO income each month!

Someone asked me, "Could Social Security ever run out of money and not be able to pay benefits?" Well, the answer is "It's possible, but very unlikely."

The reason I say it is possible is because it almost happened in 1983. The Social Security System was only several months away from bankruptcy. If Congress and the president had not acted, no checks would have been mailed out! I think we would all agree that that was a *real* crisis.

President Ronald Reagan and House Speaker Tip O'Neill along with other leaders began to pound out a solution that would eventually cut benefits and raise taxes. Now, that was an interesting combination—raise taxes and cut benefits!

One of the most significant aspects of the 1983 legislation was that Social Security began running a large annual surplus because more money was coming in than going out.

Due to having a surplus over the last twenty-plus years, the Social Security Trust Fund currently (2005) has a balance of $1.7 trillion available to be used when needed. (Don't become too excited, though, because this surplus is really unavailable, as Alarming Fact #6 will show.) The Social Security Trust Fund amount is projected to increase even more until 2017. This leads us to our next alarming fact.

ALARMING FACT #5

Rate of Return

I recently came across a 1999 GAO (Government Accountability Office) report documenting Social Security and various investment vehicle rates of return.[2] According to this report:

- Present retirees, depending on their wage earnings, can expect a return of about 4 percent.
- Historical inflation-adjusted stock market returns have averaged 7 to 8 percent during the past seventy years.
- Long-term corporate bonds have averaged 2 to 3 percent.
- Government securities have averaged 0 to 2 percent.

Not only was I surprised at the low rates of return for present retirees, but I was equally surprised to discover that historically higher-wage earners receive the lowest return, while low-wage earners end up with the highest returns.

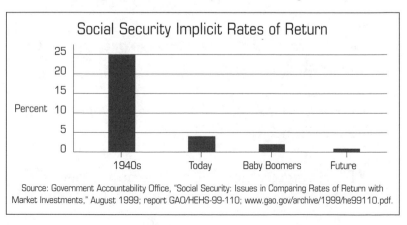

Social Security Implicit Rates of Return

Source: Government Accountability Office, "Social Security: Issues in Comparing Rates of Return with Market Investments," August 1999; report GAO/HEHS-99-110; www.gao.gov/archive/1999/he99110.pdf.

Earlier retirees in the 1940s who had paid in very little received a rate of return of 25 percent annually. Estimates are that retirees today will average about 4 percent, baby boomers can expect about 2 percent, and those born forty years from now can expect about 1 percent.[3] The report pointed out that this decline in rates is a natural result of a maturing pay-as-you-go system.

In this same GAO report (GAO/HEHS-99-110, p. 27), the following data illustrated the implicit rates of return for low, average, high, and maximum taxable income earners.

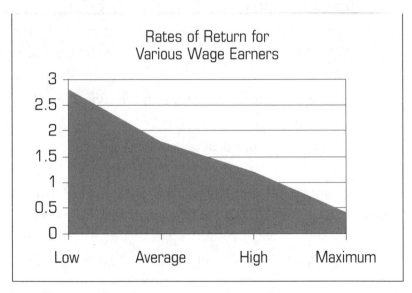

Here is what each category can expect to receive as a rate of return:

- Low-wage earner: 2.8 percent

- Average-wage earner: 1.8 percent

- High-wage earner: 1.2 percent

- Maximum-wage earner: 0.4 percent

I realize that very few workers will be earning the same amount during their forty-five working years. However, for the sake of simplicity, let's assume the following:

Annual earnings: $50,000

Payroll tax: Total 12.4%

If a worker earned $50,000, $6,200 would be paid in payroll taxes each year ($50,000 x 12.4% = $6,200). The total amount paid into the Social Security Trust Fund would be $279,000 ($6,200 x 45 years = $279,000).

If this were invested during the working years and received a return of 3 percent annually, this investment account would be worth $574,863. If after retirement the investment kept earning 3 percent, the retiree could withdraw $17,245 annually, without ever using one penny of the principal. If this money were invested during the working years and returned 6 percent, that account would be worth $1,319,000. If after retirement the investment kept earning 6 percent, the retiree could withdraw $79,140 annually, without ever using one penny of the principal. Much more on this topic later in the book.

ALARMING FACT #6

THERE IS NO MONEY IN THE SOCIAL SECURITY TRUST FUND

Why? The government spends every penny of it each year and sticks a paper IOU in the trust fund filing cabinet! This one is so alarming that I am going to devote an entire chapter to the "infamous trust fund" later in the book. Let me give you a little preview of the questions I will be answering in that chapter:

- Is there really a trust fund?
- Is there any money in the trust fund?
- How can the government spend Social Security surplus money each year?
- How is the Social Security annual surplus used to reduce the federal deficit?
- When will the trust fund go broke? Or will it?

The information on the "infamous trust fund" is one chapter you don't want to miss!

ALARMING FACT #7

THE COMING CRISIS

Since 1983, more money has been coming into the Social Security Trust Fund each year than we need to pay benefits. Therefore, we have had twenty-two consecutive years of surplus building in the Social Security Trust Fund. That amount is over $1.7 trillion.

Let's look at four critical dates anyone who seeks to understand the future of Social Security needs to know about.

2008: SURPLUS BEGINS DECLINE

In 2008, cash surpluses in the Social Security Trust Fund will begin to decline. We will still have a surplus each year, but the amount will be less than the year before. In other words, the downward spiral begins in 2008, only three years from now.

2017: Deficits Begin

In 2017, we will begin paying out more money each year than we are collecting in payroll taxes. The annual surpluses since 1983 will have vanished, and the annual deficits will begin.

In order to have enough money to pay promised benefits, the Social Security Trust Fund will then need to begin using "interest" being received on the bonds each year along with the payroll taxes being collected.

2027: Deficits Continue,
Bond Redemption Begins

In 2027 the Social Security Trust Fund will need to begin redeeming bonds—cashing in the bonds—in addition to collecting payroll tax revenue and using interest on the bonds in order to pay promised benefits.

2041: Trust Fund Depleted

In 2041 the Social Security Trust Fund will be 100 percent depleted—no more bonds available to cash in, no more interest to be earned.

At this point, according to SSA projections, the annual money coming into the system will be able to pay about 74 percent of the promised benefits. Let me be very clear on this point. The trust fund will be empty, but 74 percent of benefits will still be able to be paid each month. Why? Because payroll taxes will continue to

A MEDICARE FLASH . . .

Medicare, a key healthcare benefits program that is administered by the SSA under a separate fund, has some key dates of its own:

- **2004:** Medicare began paying more in benefits than it was taking in, and deficits will grow rapidly beginning in 2011.[4]
- **2020:** The Medicare Trust Fund (HI) will be 100 percent depleted.[5]
- **2024:** Projected expenses for Medicare will surpass Social Security expenditures.

Medicare's financial outlook has deteriorated dramatically over the past five years and is now much worse than that of Social Security.[6] The remedies proposed at present seem severe. In their *Summary of 2005 Annual Report for Social Security and Medicare,* the trustees suggested Medicare A could be brought into actuarial balance for the next seventy-five years by (1) immediate 107 percent increase in program income, or (2) immediate 48 percent reduction in program outlays, or (3) some combination of both.

be deducted from workers' paychecks each month, taxes that will cover 74 percent of Social Security benefits. (The Congressional Budget Office projects the Social Security Trust Fund depletion date to be 2052, not 2041.)

There you have it—seven alarming facts I discovered about Social Security that everyone needs to understand. But don't forget that we have not addressed in detail the infamous Social Security Trust Fund. This topic will receive special attention in chapter 4. Earlier, in chapter 3, I will be addressing "the problems" with Social Security. In other words, why the system is going broke.

Before we move on to the next chapter, let's review what we have learned about Social Security. Go ahead and take the quiz, and see how much you remember! Each quiz will help you focus on some of the major points in this chapter. *Have fun.*

NOTES
· ·

1. "Social Security Basic Facts," www.ssa.gov/pressoffice/basicfact.htm

2. General Accountability Office, "Social Security: Issues in Comparing Rates of Return with Market Investments," August 1999, 4, report GAO/HEHS-99-110; www./gao.gov/archive/1999/hr99110.pdf

3. Ibid., 6.

4. Government Accountability Office, "Social Security Reform: Early Action Would Be Prudent," 9 March 2005, 9, report GAO-05-397T; www.gao.gov/new.items/d05397t.pdf.

5. Projections for 2020 and 2024 results are from "A Summary of the 2005 Annual Reports, Social Security and Medicare Boards of Trustees," www.ssa.gov/OACT/TRSUM/trsummary.html

6. Medicare deficits already began appearing in 2004, even though the 2000 Summary Report for Social Security and Medicare projected Medicare deficits to begin no sooner than 2010.

SOCIAL SECURITY KNOWLEDGE QUIZ

1. In what year was the Social Security Act signed into legislation?
   (a) 1897   (c) 1935
   (b) 1920   (d) 1962

2. The money you pay into Social Security this year . . .
   (a) is placed in a Social Security account with your name on it.
   (b) is invested in stocks and bonds.
   (c) is used this year to pay benefits for those already retired.
   (d) will never be seen again.

3. The *average* monthly benefit for a retired worker is:
   (a) $562 per month
   (b) $955 per month
   (c) $1,985 per month
   (d) $2,400 per month

4. The *maximum* monthly benefit for a worker (if Bill Gates was age sixty-five and retired this year, how much would his monthly benefit check be?):
   (a) $562 per month
   (b) $942 per month
   (c) $1,784 per month
   (d) $19,677 per month

5. What is the maximum amount of wages taxed for Social Security in 2005?
   (a) $50,000   (c) $140,000
   (b) $90,000   (d) No limit

6. What is the maximum amount of wages taxed for Medicare?
   (a) $50,000   (c) $140,000
   (b) $90,000   (d) No limit

7. What percentage of those over age sixty-five depend on SS for 100 percent of their income?
   (a) 10%
   (b) 22%
   (c) 40%
   (d) 75%

8. In what year did Social Security begin running a surplus and has continued to do so ever since?
   (a) 1935
   (b) 1962
   (c) 1983
   (d) 1995

9. In what year is it projected that Social Security will no longer have a surplus and will need to begin using interest being earned on the special treasury bonds in the Social Security Trust Fund?
   (a) 2008
   (b) 2017
   (c) 2028
   (d) 2042

10. In what year is it projected that Social Security will deplete the trust fund and have to cut benefits to 74 percent (unless changes are made before then)?
   (a) 2008
   (b) 2018
   (c) 2028
   (d) 2041

Turn to page 176 and check your answers.

THE TOP TEN
HALF-TRUTHS

What am I not being told?

AS I HAVE DILIGENTLY researched and talked with people of all ages, I have discovered many people have read or been told something about Social Security that is only partially true. Let's go ahead and call it a "half-truth." There might be some truth, but it's certainly not the whole truth.

Have you ever heard a coworker boldly proclaim, "I don't see why we have to pay into Social Security because no one in Congress has to pay into the program. Not even the president pays into the system. They realize the program is so pathetic that they have their own retirement plan"?

Or maybe you have heard a friend say, "I'm afraid there is not going to be any money left in the program when I retire."

In this chapter I plan to set the record straight, give you the whole truth, and do my best to explain the facts surrounding each half-truth.

Let me begin by addressing the two examples that I gave above, which I call half-truths 1 and 2.

HALF-TRUTH #1

MEMBERS OF CONGRESS, FEDERAL AND STATE EMPLOYEES DO NOT HAVE TO PAY INTO SOCIAL SECURITY.

The fact is the president, vice president, all members of Congress, federal judges, and most political appointees began to be covered under the Social Security program beginning in 1984. Prior to that time most federal employees were not paying into the Social Security system but had their own retirement plan. The majority of those who still do not pay into Social Security are state and local government employees who are covered by their own retirement system. Military personnel have been covered since 1957.

Federal employees, including members of Congress, are offered a voluntary retirement savings plan called TSP: Thrift Savings Plan. This is in addition to Social Security.

The statement is a *half-truth* because before 1984, it is accurate; most federal employees were not participants in the Social Security System; and even today many state and local government employees still are not in the program.

SOCIAL SECURITY WILL NOT HAVE ANY MONEY BY THE TIME I RETIRE.

One Saturday morning my wife, my son, and I were driving to a high school state track meet. As I was telling them about some of my Social Security research, Austin asked, "Dad, will Social Security even be around when I am seventy?" Austin's question identified the thoughts of most young people today who have taken the time to even think about Social Security.

The thinking that Social Security will run out of money is a *half-truth* because as long as the United States government continues to deduct payroll taxes there will be some money available to pay benefits. It is possible that benefits will be reduced, but some benefits will be paid. This half-truth is closely related to #3.

SOCIAL SECURITY IS CLOSE TO GOING BANKRUPT.

In order to respond to this half-truth, we need to define "close" and "bankrupt." Is *close* next year, or could it be viewed as forty years later? Presently the Social Security Trust Fund has a surplus of $1.7 trillion. (Much more on the trust fund in chapter 4.) However, the trust fund is projected to be 100 percent depleted in 2041. That's thirty-six years from now. In addition, in 2041, the payroll taxes would be able to cover 74 percent of the promised benefits as long as payroll taxes are being deducted.

THE AVERAGE PERSON WILL NEVER RECEIVE BACK ALL THE MONEY HE PAID INTO THE SYSTEM.

This statement is true for some, but not true for everyone. If you (and/or your spouse) live for *many* years beyond the age of sixty-five, it is very likely that you will collect in benefits more than you paid in. However, if you and your spouse were to die before you reach age sixty-five or a few years after, you would receive no benefits or very little benefits.

Until recent years, Social Security recipients received more—often far more—than the value of the Social Security taxes they paid. However, because Social Security tax rates have increased over the years and the age for full benefits is scheduled to rise, it is becoming increasingly apparent that Social Security will be less of a good deal for many future recipients. "For example, for workers who earned average wages and retired in 1980 at age 65, it took 2.8 years to recover the value of the retirement portion of the combined employee and employer shares of their Social Security taxes plus interest. For their counterparts who retired at age 65 in 2003, it will take 17.4 years. For those retiring in 2020, it will take 21.6 years (based on the trustees' 2003 intermediate forecast). Some observers believe these discrepancies are inequitable and cite them as evidence that the system needs to be substantially restructured."[1]

39 . . . . The Top Ten Half-Truths

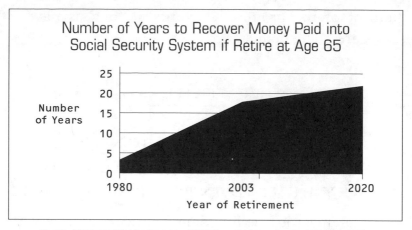

Number of Years to Recover Money Paid into Social Security System if Retire at Age 65

Number of Years

25
20
15
10
5
0

1980   2003   2020

Year of Retirement

Source: CRS Issue Brief for Congress; Social Security Reform, Updated 21 April, 2005.

"An average earner born in 1915 and turning 65 in 1980 could expect to get back roughly $60,000 more than he paid into the system (adjusted for inflation and interest). Someone born in 1936 will just about break even, and those born after 1960 can expect to pay at least $30,000 more in payroll taxes than they ever receive in benefits."[2]

The truth is . . . it all depends on when you were born, how much you paid in, and how long you live!

HALF-TRUTH #5

SOCIAL SECURITY IS AN INSURANCE PROGRAM.

Some view Social Security as an insurance program. Some documents even call it insurance. Legally, there is no guarantee that those paying payroll taxes will receive retirement benefits in the future. If you and your spouse die at age sixty-two, your family (under most circumstances) would receive nothing. That's right, nothing! But you do have disability and survivors insurance if you were to need it before you turn sixty-five. And you have "retirement insurance" that will pay if you live long enough to collect it. In some ways, it's like term insurance. If you need it, it pays. If you don't need it or don't live long enough to collect retirement benefits, it never pays. Therefore, it is a form of insurance for some benefits, and not insurance for other benefits.

HALF-TRUTH #6

SOCIAL SECURITY NUMBERS WERE DESIGNED TO CLASSIFY PEOPLE BY RACE.

It is true that the middle two numbers are known as your "group number," but group numbers are not intended to indicate racial groupings. For example,

555 55 5555

The two middle numbers were designed to help with the organization and manual filing of thousands of

Courtesy of the Social Security Administration

Social Security cards in filing cabinets. This subgroup number helped in this administrative process.

Social Security records were originally kept in thousands of filing cabinets and card files like the ones in the above scene from the Candler Building in the late 1930s.

HALF-TRUTH #7

SOCIAL SECURITY IS "ONLY" A RETIREMENT PROGRAM.

Social Security is a retirement program, but not just a retirement program. Here is a list of the various benefits provided by the Social Security program:

- *Retirement benefits.* For worker, spouse, and child (with specific qualifications). For example, when a worker retires and if they have children under eighteen (or under nineteen and in high school), the child would also receive benefits.
- *Survivors Benefits.* For spouse and children of a worker who dies (with specific qualifications).
- *Disability Benefits.* For workers who become disabled and their spouse and children (with specific qualifications).
- *Medicare.* Health insurance for those over age sixty-five. Part A is hospital insurance. Part B is medical insurance (has a monthly premium). Part D is prescription drugs.[3]

The Social Security program is sometimes known as OASDHI: Old Age, Survivors, Disability, and Health Insurance. Thus, it is a retirement program, but not just a retirement program.

HALF-TRUTH #8

MEDICARE IS NOT A PART OF SOCIAL SECURITY.

Medicare came about in 1965 when Congress amended the Social Security Act of 1935 to include health insurance for the retired worker. So technically speaking, Medicare is a part of Social Security, but the funds to cover Social Security and Medicare are kept separate.

HALF-TRUTH #9

SOCIAL SECURITY TRUST FUND MONEY IS IN A "LOCKBOX."

When people use the term "lockbox," they are implying that the Social Security surplus money should be kept in the trust fund and not spent by the federal government. It is true that surplus trust fund money is not in a lockbox, but it is protected and guaranteed by the federal government. The federal government uses the surplus each year and puts in an IOU to be paid back in the future. (See chapter 4 for much more information on the infamous trust fund.)

SOCIAL SECURITY IS A SOCIALISTIC WELFARE PROGRAM.

To be a socialistic welfare program (in the strictest definition), the government would have to take from the rich and transfer this wealth to the poor. Social Security does neither. Rich and poor are taxed alike—at the same payroll tax rate. In addition, rich and poor each receive monthly benefits regardless of their net worth. However, we have noted that 22 percent of those over the age of sixty-five depend on Social Security for their only source of income. So you could say that the program in some form is a welfare program for the needy.

The longstanding "equality" aspect (everyone is treated the same) of Social Security might be changing in the future. One proposal on the table being discussed is called progressive indexing, which would allow benefits for lower-income workers to grow faster than benefits for higher-income workers. (See chapter 6 for more information.)

"GIVE US THE REAL FACTS"

I hope this chapter helped you to understand the half-truths out there about Social Security and provided you with helpful documentation concerning each one.

As I have talked with numerous senior citizens, groups, and friends, they want to know, "Are there real problems with the Social Security program?" And if there are problems, "Give us the documentation. Give us the real facts. Give us the truth!"

In the next chapter, I will summarize the problems with Social Security into six major categories. But, first, let's see how much you learned from this chapter! Please complete Social Security Knowledge Quiz 2.

NOTES
. . . .

1. CRS Issue Brief for Congress: "Social Security Reform," IB98048, Updated 21 April 2005; 6–7; http://fpc.state.gov/documents/organization/45974.pdf

2. *U.S. News & World Report,* 20 April 1998, 24.

3. Part C of Medicare, created in the mid-1960s as an alternative to Parts A and B, includes inpatient hospital care (Part A) and physician services and outpatient care (Part B) but provides these coverages through a health maintenance organization, preferred provider organization, medical savings account, or other new type of health plan. Part C is intended to utilize cost-saving measures through managed care, controlling a rising deductible in Part A and rising premiums in Part B.

1. Which of the following do not pay into Social Security?
   (a) The president of the United States
   (b) Congress
   (c) Federal judges
   (d) None of the above

2. What would have to take place before Social Security would have zero dollars to pay out in benefits?
   (a) The trust fund will have to be depleted 100 percent.
   (b) Congress will have to raise taxes.
   (c) Retirement age must be raised.
   (d) Payroll taxes must be 100 percent eliminated.

3. If nothing changes between now and 2041, what percent of current benefits will Social Security be able to pay beginning in 2041?
   (a) 0%   (c) 74%
   (b) 25%   (d) 100%

4. Under what circumstance is it possible for neither you nor your spouse to receive any retirement benefits (assuming you are covered)?
   (a) If you both live to be one hundred.
   (b) If you both die before the age of sixty-two.
   (c) If one of you dies before sixty-two, and one dies at age sixty-seven.
   (d) If you have children after you are seventy-five years old.

5. The middle numbers in your Social Security number:
   (a) Are used for race identification.
   (b) Are used for nationality identification.
   (c) Initially helped workers file Social Security cards.
   (d) Are used to identify your ideal weight.

6. Social Security covers:
   (a) Retirement benefits.
   (b) Survivor benefits.
   (c) Disability benefits.
   (d) All of the above.

7. Social Security surplus money each year is:
   (a) Kept in a "lockbox."
   (b) Used to subsidize pay for professional athletes.
   (c) Spent each year by the federal government.
   (d) Invested in the stock market.

8. There will always be money for Social Security to pay
   some benefits as long as:
   (a) The Democrats are in control.
   (b) The Republicans are in control.
   (c) The bond interest rate is greater than 3 percent.
   (d) The government keeps deducting payroll taxes.

9. Medicare funds are:
   (a) Kept in the Social Security Trust Fund.
   (b) Kept in a separate trust fund from the Social Security
       Trust Fund.
   (c) Invested in health mutual funds and stocks.
   (d) Used by health insurance companies to hire young
       attorneys to fight malpractice claims.

10. Why is Social Security not a socialistic welfare program?
    (a) Rich and poor are taxed at the same rate.
    (b) Everyone receives benefits regardless of their net worth.
    (c) Both (a) and (b).
    (d) Social welfare ended in 1935.

CHAPTER 3

THE PROBLEMS

What went wrong, or did it?

RECENTLY I WAS SPEAKING to a group of people on the topic of Social Security. A key part of my presentation was to identify and explain (in less than twenty minutes) the underlying problems with Social Security (if any). Now, that's the kind of assignment I just love. Give me a complex topic and enough time to research it, and I will summarize the data and give you the basic facts (with charts)!

In this chapter I will be giving you a synopsis of what I communicated that day in my presentation.

The words of Nobel economist Paul Samuelson printed in a 1998 edition of *U.S News & World Report* still ring true: "It [Social Security] is actuarially unsound. . . . It relies on a growing population and rising incomes to pay each generation of retirees more than they paid into the system."[1] To understand the problems with Social Security, we must examine its initial structure or setup.

It is my opinion that some fundamental features or principles were not properly put into place back in 1935 when the initial legislation was passed.

Here's the fundamental problem: President Roosevelt needed to begin paying benefits to senior citizens and those in need IMMEDIATELY—not in thirty-five years! There was no time for funds to accrue in an account with their names on it. The only way to accomplish paying benefits immediately was to create a "pay-as-you-go" system. (See Alarming Fact #1 in chapter 1 for more details.)

I am fairly confident that President Roosevelt never would have proposed or agreed to legislation that was calling for 3.3 workers to have the responsibility to fund retirement benefits for one retiree, as is true today. In 1945, the year Roosevelt died, forty-two workers were paying into the system for each retiree. He would understand that the tax load would create a huge burden for each worker.

Over the years we've had opportunities to correct the course, but have continually failed to do so. Congress could correct the problem at any time—but they have not been willing to do so.

I believe most experts on Social Security would agree that it's not just one area that is creating the problem, but a combination of several.

The entire Social Security system was built upon some basic assumptions. Many of these assumptions are no longer true, but the system is still operating on them. Problems have developed in place of these assumptions. Each problem can be solved. The question is, Are we willing to do what it takes to solve them?

INCREASING LIFE EXPECTANCY

When Social Security began in 1935, the average life expectancy "at birth" was sixty-one years. The benefits were scheduled to begin at age sixty-five. It doesn't take the smartest kid in the class to figure this one out.

I can just imagine what it would be like teaching this material in a high school personal finance class. I would love to cover this point without making a comment, pause to look at my notes, and just wait to see what some kid might say!

I hope that someone might say, "Mr. Pope, most people would be dead before they had an opportunity to receive their first check!"

Then I would laugh and say, "You're absolutely right. Now tell me your name, because you are going to receive an A for today's lesson!"

Those folks back in 1935 when they passed this legislation were a lot sharper than we give them credit for.

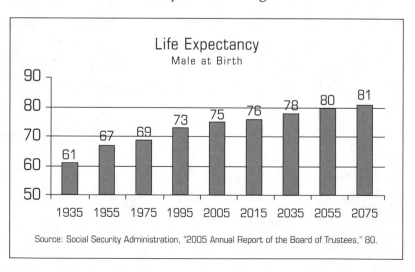

Source: Social Security Administration, "2005 Annual Report of the Board of Trustees," 80.

As the "Life Expectancy" chart shows, people are living longer, an average age (for males) of seventy-five years in 2005, and the age will trend upward. Let's briefly lay out the long-term ramifications of how people living longer impacts the current Social Security program.

The longer people live:

- The more monthly benefit checks they will receive.
- The greater number of people we will have in retirement.
- The increased financial strain it creates in the program.
- The more money workers need to pay into the system.

Therefore, an initial problem with Social Security was that Congress did not tie retirement age to a life expectancy chart but "fixed it at age sixty-five." Congress did make a small adjustment back in 1983 when they established a timetable to gradually increase the retirement age to sixty-seven. (See table 2, column 3, in appendix B.)

Meanwhile, death rates have continued to decline. For those 65 and over, "between 1979 and 2001 the age-sex-adjusted death rate . . . declined at an average annual rate of 0.47 percent," reports the Social Security Board of Trustees.[2] Death rates have declined due to (1) growing medical knowledge, (2) better health care services, (3) improved nutrition, and (4) improved sanitation.

Because people are living longer, this creates a second major problem.

WORKER-TO-RETIREE RATIO

In 1945, forty-two workers were paying into the system for every one retiree. That's forty-two people working for every one person retired! Each worker had to pay approximately 2.38 percent of each retiree's benefit.

Today, in 2005, 3.3 workers must support one retiree. The percentage of benefits that one worker has to pay for one retiree is 30.3 percent! It is projected in 2040 that this ratio will become 2 to 1. This will increase the worker's percentage to 50 percent unless (1) there are Social Security trust funds available to subsidize, (2) funding from the general budget is available, (3) benefits are decreased, or (4) the federal government borrows more money.

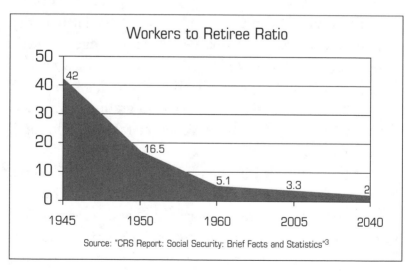

We can only assume that in one hundred years or more, the worker-to-retiree ratio will become 1 to 1. Each worker will be supporting his/her very own retiree. Maybe the government could begin to administrate a program where the worker would receive a picture and bio of their very own retiree! Kind of like an "adopt-a-senior plan." The retiree would receive a picture of their worker to put on the refrigerator! And maybe on special occasions like the worker's birthday, the retiree could send the worker some homemade cookies. They could also exchange family pictures. The worker could send a picture of him/her at work (in a bank or construction job), and the retiree could send pictures of them playing golf, watching TV, playing bingo, or on the beach with the grandkids.

Of course, I am kidding about this, but we have to find some humor in the situation. Or maybe we don't need to find any humor in the situation. You decide.

PROBLEM #3

DECLINING FERTILITY RATE

It's a fact that Americans are not having as many children. We are just under the sustainable birth rate of 2.10. If it were not for immigration, the population in America would be declining.

Fertility rate is defined as the average number of children who would be born to a woman in her childbearing years (between ages fourteen and forty-nine).

After booming during the postwar years of 1946 to 1964—from a birth rate of 2.23 children in 1940 to 3.61 in 1960—annual birth rates dropped noticeably, declining to 1.77 children in 1975. Since 1990 fertility rates have averaged about 2.00 children per woman. Fertility rates are projected during the long term to remain close to present levels. Trends that will continue to affect fer-

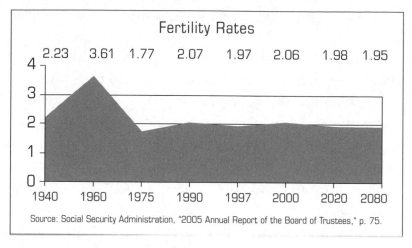

Fertility Rates

2.23	3.61	1.77	2.07	1.97	2.06	1.98	1.95

1940   1960   1975   1990   1997   2000   2020   2080

tility rates are: (1) rising percentage of women who never marry, (2) women who are divorced, (3) number of young women in labor force, (4) use of birth control to ensure smaller families, and (5) abortion.

Fewer babies being born translates into fewer workers paying into Social Security.

PROBLEM #4

LOSS OF WORKERS
DUE TO ABORTION

Let's take a closer look at the last reason listed in trends affecting fertility rates: elective abortion; i.e., the deliberate termination of a pregnancy (for nonmedical reasons). According to the Alan Guttmacher Institute, an agency devoted to sexual and reproductive health research and policy analysis, approximately 1.37 million abortions occur in the United States each year.[4] This would mean that since the 1973 Supreme Court ruling that legalized abortion *(Roe v. Wade)*, almost forty-four million babies have been aborted. Christians and others who oppose abortion as morally and biblically wrong could easily cite another damaging effect in taking the life of the unborn: It is diminishing the pool of future adults who would support retiring workers.

Due to abortion, our nation has lost millions of workers who would be paying into the Social Security Trust Fund. Assuming an average age of twenty for workers who enter the workforce, since 1993 (twenty years after *Roe v. Wade*), we would have sixteen million more workers paying into the system. And that number would be increasing by 1.37 million new workers every year! We have lost millions of workers who would be helping to get us through the baby boomer retirement years by paying into the Social Security Trust Fund.

PROBLEM #5

NOT YOUR TYPICAL PENSION PLAN

The federal government definitely has different legal standards for running their retirement program than corporate America. You could almost say that the current Social Security system is the *mother of all Ponzi schemes.* I found the following explanation of Ponzi schemes on the Securities Exchange Commission's Web site:

"Ponzi schemes are a type of illegal pyramid scheme named for Charles Ponzi, who duped thousands of New England residents into investing in a postage stamp speculation scheme back in the 1920s. . . . Decades later, the Ponzi scheme continues to work on the 'rob-Peter-to-pay-Paul' principle, as money from new investors is used to pay off earlier investors until the whole scheme collapses."[5]

The early investors always receive their investment back as promised. Where did the money come from? The money received by new investors is immediately paid to the earlier investors. It's a cash-in, cash-out system. *It's a pay-as-you-go system.* The problem is, those who are last in line usually receive nothing. The early investors get their money back, the organizer spends money from the fund, and the last ones to join end up with nothing but heartache and problems.

Let me be very clear about this point. I fully believe that the United States government will pay Social Security benefits in the future to everyone. BUT I can assure you, if this were not a program being run and backed by the United States government, the organizers would be spending the rest of their lives behind bars wearing striped pants and shirts (with numbers across the back).

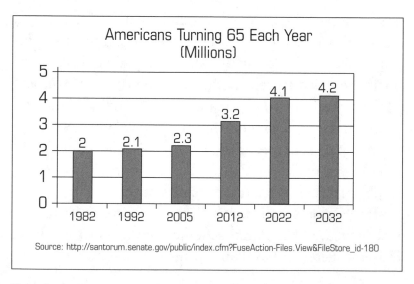

Americans Turning 65 Each Year (Millions)

Source: http://santorum.senate.gov/public/index.cfm?FuseAction-Files.View&FileStore_id-180

No business in the United States is allowed to run a pension plan for its employees the way our government is operating Social Security.

As I documented earlier, the Social Security program has made promises of $4 trillion (in today's dollars) more than projected tax revenue.

A smaller labor force (see problems #3 and #4) will only lead to a slower growth in federal revenues (i.e., less money to be taxed). This will result in increasing pressure on the federal budget in years to come.

PROBLEM #6

THE BABY BOOMERS

Today approximately 37 million people are receiving old-age benefits. However, 79 million baby boomers (those born between 1946 and 1964) will retire beginning in 2011, and those taking early retirement (age sixty-two) as soon as 2008—just three years from this writing! This will be almost double the number of people receiving Social Security checks today.

The baby boomers will soon begin putting pressure on every aspect of our society:

- Social Security benefits
- Increased healthcare costs for Medicare
- Increased pressure on the medical community
- Increased pressure on the stock market

Why the stock market? As these 79 million baby boomers begin to liquidate assets for retirement (IRAs,

401(k)s, 403(b)s, and other assets), it could potentially create a strain on the economy and especially the stock market. Too much money coming out of the market in a relatively short period of time always creates problems. This is something that cannot be overlooked.

In 2005, 37 million Americans were age sixty-five and older. By 2031, 71 million Americans will be age sixty-five and older. This represents a remarkable increase of over 92 percent in just over twenty-five years!

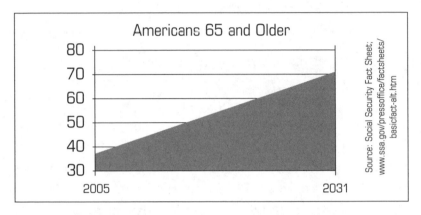

As documented earlier, as more Americans turn sixty-five, more stress is placed on the entire system. (See Table 3, Appendix B, for a history of growing numbers of Social Security beneficiaries.)

PROBLEM #7

Increasing Payroll Taxes

Since 1935, payroll taxes have been increased twenty times! When is it going to stop? How high can it go? You tell me.

In 2005, for every dollar earned in wages up to $90,000, the employee pays 6.2 percent and the employer pays 6.2 percent, for a combined total of 12.4 percent payroll tax for Social Security. This cap is adjusted each year for inflation. For example, in 2004 the cap was $87,900. (In addition, for every dollar in wages, the employee pays 1.45 percent and the employer pays 1.45 percent for a combined total of 2.9 percent for Medicare. Note: There is no salary cap on taxes for Medicare. The combined Social Security and Medicare taxes total 15.3 percent.)

The less funds we give the average worker, the less funds he or she has to purchase items, save for the

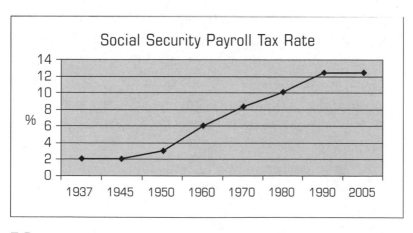

Social Security Payroll Tax Rate

future, and give to worthy causes. More taxes mean a smaller paycheck!

Payroll taxes are already a burden to business owners—especially small business owners.

SOCIAL SECURITY FLASHBACK

A 1936 pamphlet promised that 3 percent is "the most you will ever pay" in Social Security taxes. (www.ssa.gov/history/ssb36.html)

PROBLEM #8

WELFARE MIND-SET

There appears to be an attitude that it's the responsibility of the federal government to provide and take care of people when they reach the age of retirement. Let's be fair to the workers who have been paying Social Security taxes their entire working life; they should expect something in return. But what attitude does the current system communicate? Individual or government responsibility? Does the current system create any sense of personal responsibility for its citizens?

Is it the government's responsibility to provide for the welfare of its senior citizens? (We will discuss this in chapter 8.)

PROBLEM #9

SOLVENCY ISSUE

As I have documented earlier, Social Security does have a long-term solvency issue that needs to be addressed immediately.

In a May 6, 2005, letter, the comptroller general of the United States issued his own "financial alert." (I have added italics to help highlight some of his points.)

"As you know, the Social Security system faces serious solvency and sustainability challenges in the longer term. While the Social Security program does not face an immediate crisis, it does have a *$4 trillion gap* between promised and funded benefits in current dollar terms over the next 75 years. This gap is growing as time passes, and given this and other major fiscal challenges, including expected growth in federal health spending, it would be prudent to act sooner rather than later to reform the Social Security program.

"Furthermore, Social Security's finances have important *implications for the overall federal budget,*" the comptroller general explained. Once the SS surpluses begin to decline, the federal budget will come under greater pressure. "In addition, Social Security will start running a *cash flow deficit in 2017,* which will require the federal government to either *increase federal taxes, cut other federal spending,* or *borrow additional funds* from the public in order to redeem bonds in the Social Security trust funds.

"Failure to take steps to address our large and structural long-range fiscal imbalance, which is driven in large part by projected increases in Medicare, Medicaid, and Social Security spending, will *ultimately have significant adverse consequences* for our future economy and the quality of life of our children, grandchildren, and future generations of Americans."[6]

The comptroller general's warning of a fiscal imbalance, driven by projected increases in Social Security, Medicare, and Medicaid, prompts me to issue the following financial alert:

FINANCIAL ALERT

Our nation is faced with long-term fiscal imbalance, which, if ignored, will result in a financial meltdown beginning in the United States and spreading around the world.

You are asking, "How can you say this?"

This is another one of those times that if we were sitting across the table from each other, I would stand up, look you directly in your eyes, and say, **"How can a person not be shouting 'Financial Alert!' in the public arena when it is projected in 2050 that Social Security, Medicare, and Medicaid will consume 75 percent of the federal budget?"**

The chart below shows that Social Security, Medicare, and other trust funds accounted for 45 percent of the federal budget in 2003, leaving 55 percent for all other government expenses (defense, education, etc.). By 2050, spending for entitlement programs is projected to consume 75 percent of the federal budget, leaving only 25 percent for the rest of our nation's needs.

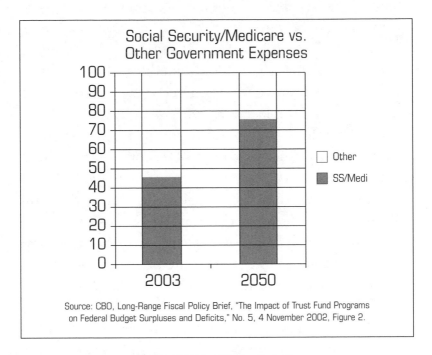

Source: CBO, Long-Range Fiscal Policy Brief, "The Impact of Trust Fund Programs on Federal Budget Surpluses and Deficits," No. 5, 4 November 2002, Figure 2.

PROBLEM #10

SEVENTY-FIVE YEAR ACTUARIAL PERIOD

For years SSA officials have used a period of seventy-five years to evaluate the long-term financial outlook of Social Security and to evaluate any potential reform in the program. For example, in 2004, the Social Security board of trustees did an evaluation for the years 2005–2080.

While this procedure is somewhat acceptable when the program is running a surplus or occasional deficits, it is totally unacceptable when the program is running growing deficits in the future.

Here is the reason. If you come up with a solution to solve the problem for the next seventy-five years, the very next year, insolvency becomes a valid issue again. That's because in the seventy-five-year time frame you used this year, 2005–2080, the following year will become 2006–2081. Therefore the seventy-five-year time frame has eliminated a large surplus year (2005) and has replaced it with a large deficit year (2081). Therefore, the solution you just agreed to several months ago to solve the problem, no longer solves the problem.

What we need is a solution that not only solves the problem for the next seventy-five years, but permanently. In order to accomplish this, we need to devise a plan that will transition us from a pay-as-you-go system.

If the government wanted to completely fund Social Security for the next seventy-five years, it would require that Congress come up with $5.7 trillion dollars today. This includes the $1.7 trillion owed the trust fund and an additional $4 trillion to make up the shortfall between projected payroll taxes and promised benefits. If SSA wanted to fund the "perpetual projection" that extends beyond the normal seventy-five-year planning horizon, it would require $12.8 trillion in today's dollars. This amount would cover the $1.7 already owed to the trust fund and $11.1 trillion of future obligations.

As I will explain later, I believe part of the permanent solution will involve some form of private accounts. As you realize, this is one option being debated in our nation today.

Now for another review and your third Social Security exam. Before you read the next chapter, take a few minutes and see how much you have learned about the problems of Social Security.

NOTES
· ·

1. *U.S. News & World Report,* 20 April 1998, 24.

2. Social Security Administration, "The 2005 Annual Report of the Board of Trustees of the Federal Old-Age & Survivors Insurance & Disability Insurance Trust Funds," 5 April 2005, 72; www.ssa.gov/OACT/TR/TR05

3. Gary Sidor, Congressional Research Service, "CRS Report: Social Security: Brief Facts and Statistics," 3 March 2005, Code 94-27, p. 10; http://fpc.state.gov/documents/organization/45222.pdf

4. Alan Guttmacher Institute, as cited on the popular Web site About.com: http://www.womensissues.about.com/cs/abortionstats/a/aaabortionstats.htm

5. www.sec.gov/answers/ponzi.htm

6. May 6, 2005, letter to The Honorable Bill Thomas, chairman, Committee on Ways and Means, House of Representatives, from David M. Walker, comptroller general of the United States, as quoted in Government Accountability Office report GAO-05-649R, 5; http://www.gao.gov/new.items/d05649r.pdf

SOCIAL SECURITY KNOWLEDGE QUIZ

1. In 1935, the year Social Security began, the life expectancy at birth was:
   (a) fifty years
   (b) sixty-one years
   (c) sixty-seven years
   (d) seventy-seven years

2. In 2005 the average life expectancy at birth is:
   (a) fifty years
   (b) sixty-one years
   (c) sixty-seven years
   (d) seventy-five years

3. In 1945 the workers-to-retiree ratio was:
   (a) 1,000 workers for every 1 retiree
   (b) 42 workers for every 1 retiree
   (c) 3.3 workers for every 1 retiree
   (d) 1 worker for every 1 retiree

4. In 2005 the workers-to-retiree ratio is:
   (a) 1000 workers for every 1 retiree
   (b) 42 workers for every 1 retiree
   (c) 3.3 workers for every 1 retiree
   (d) 1 worker for every 1 retiree

5. In 2040 the workers-to-retiree ratio is projected to be:
   (a) 42 workers for every 1 retiree
   (b) 20 workers for every 1 retiree
   (c) 2 workers for every 1 retiree
   (d) 1 worker for every 1 retiree

6. In a Ponzi scheme:
   (a) Early investors usually receive money, and last investors receive nothing.
   (b) No one receives any money.
   (c) Everyone receives a small return on their investment.
   (d) Everyone receives double their money invested.

7. The 79 million baby boomers are people born between the years:
   (a) 1910 and 1929
   (b) 1930 and 1939
   (c) 1946 and 1964
   (d) 1975 and 1999

8. What is one of the major problems with our analysis of Social Security?
   (a) We don't factor in the unemployment rate.
   (b) We use a seventy-five-year horizon, which becomes invalid the very next year.
   (c) We have too much money in the trust fund.
   (d) It does not allow enough monthly income for people to go on expensive vacations each year.

9. Since 1935, payroll taxes have been increased how many times?
   (a) none
   (b) three times
   (c) twenty times
   (d) annually

10. A fundamental question that is being debated today is:
    (a) Should we discontinue the Social Security program?
    (b) Should we privatize a portion of Social Security?
    (c) Should we add on more benefits and help more people?
    (d) Should we transfer the administration of Social Security to the FBI?

CHAPTER 4

THE INFAMOUS TRUST FUND

Where's the money?

DO YOU REMEMBER back in the 1970s when Wendy's ran a very popular commercial with the punch line "Where's the beef?"

A little old lady would walk up to the counter of a fast food restaurant and order a hamburger. When they put the order on the counter, the hamburger consisted of a small piece of meat on a very large bun. She would look down at the hamburger, look up at the person standing behind the counter, and ask sarcastically, "Where's the beef?"

One of the most important questions Americans should be asking concerning Social Security should be "Where's the beef?" Or better yet, "Where's the money?"

The SSA estimates that if we make no changes in our current system, benefit checks will shrink to approximately 74 percent of the promised benefits in 2041.[1]

If you listen to any news reports or read any articles or know practically anything about Social Security, you have heard about the Social Security Trust Fund. The infamous fund is one of the most misunderstood aspects of the coming Social Security crisis. I use the word *crisis* because I believe *how* the trust funds are being used *today* will create a crisis in the *future*.

A Little History and a Few Definitions

From 1935 to 2005, the amount of money collected in Social Security payroll taxes has exceeded the amount being paid out in benefits every year except for eleven years—fifty-nine out of seventy years.

Here are some common terms, with their definitions, that are used to described the present and future operation of the Social Security Trust Fund:

- *Surplus.* Each year when payroll taxes (income) exceed benefits being paid out (expenses), this creates what we call a surplus.

- *Deficit.* Each year when benefits being paid out (expenses) exceed payroll taxes (income), this creates what we call a deficit. The last year Social Security ran a deficit was in 1981. The SSA projects Social Security will continue to run a surplus (but declining each year) until 2017.

- *The Trust Fund.* Every year that we have a surplus, the money is deposited into the Social Security

Trust Fund. In 2004, the surplus deposited into the Social Security Trust Fund was $156 billion. Also, at the end of 2004 the balance in the trust fund was $1.7 trillion.

- *Trust Fund Assets (Balance).* Since the beginning in 1935, the total of all the surpluses, minus the deficits, plus the earned interest, equals the trust fund assets, or balance. That is . . .

(Total of Surplus - Deficits) + Interest Earned = Trust Fund Balance

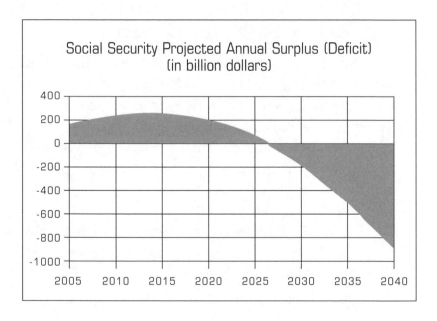

As you can see by the "Trust Fund Assets" chart (page 71), the trust fund asset value has been increasing rapidly every year since 1985. (For specific figures on the trust fund balance, see Table 1, Appendix B, which includes a long-term history of the growing trust fund balances.)

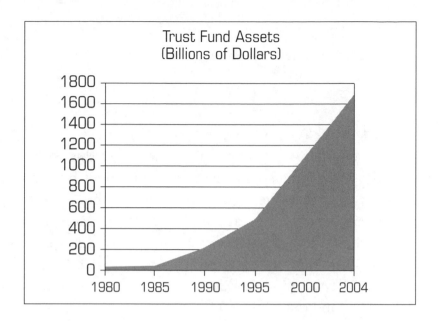

Trust Fund Assets
(Billions of Dollars)

"Where's the Trust Fund Money?"

The most common question people ask about the trust fund is, "Where *is* the Social Security Trust Fund money?" Well, that all depends upon what the definition of "is" is.

Remember in chapter 1 I promised to tell you more about the Social Security Trust Fund? Well, here are three more alarming facts! Every year that Social Security has a surplus the federal government:

- takes the money out of the fund;
- gives the trust fund a paper IOU; and
- spends 100 percent of the money.

So where "is" the money?

- 100 percent spent!

- 100 percent gone!
- 100 percent consumed!

BY WHOM?

- The federal government.

If you are like some people I know and this is the first time you understand this truth, you might be very upset at this point. Well, good for you! You should be.

But others, with great passion and conviction, will say, "Ethan, you are misleading people on this issue. The trust fund has special treasury bonds issued by the UNITED STATES OF AMERICA in the amount of $1.7 trillion . . . and the UNITED STATES OF AMERICA has never defaulted on a bond!"

Then they will go on to say with great intensity, "Ethan, those bonds in the Social Security Trust Fund are better than gold sitting in the bank!"

If I were sitting across the table from someone who just said that, here is what I would do. I would stand up, lean over the table, look him right in the eye, and with great passion say,

- "Baloney!"
- "Rubbish!"
- "Nonsense!"

Have I made myself clear?

The Social Security Trust Fund could be identified as a UFO. Not an Unidentified Flying Object, but an Unfilled Financial Obligation to the American people to keep the Social Security Trust Fund secure. Congress began taking monies out of the Social Security Trust Fund back in 1968, putting IOUs in their place. That's almost forty years of spending trust fund resources.

Why am I taking such a strong stance? Sure, the Social Security Trust Fund has special treasury bonds, but when they need to be paid back, HOW will they be paid?

At great cost to the American people!

Since the money has already been spent, the federal government can only come up with the money to repay the debt (IOUs) in one of three ways (or a combination of the three):

1. Reduce federal spending by cutting government programs like defense, education, homeland security, food stamps, healthcare, and other programs.

2. Borrow money from someone else to pay off the debt—and as a result, increase the national debt. All this would do is borrow trillions of dollars more from Americans or foreign nations to pay back the trust fund. The national debt in June of 2005 was already $7.8 trillion. That's $7,800,000,000,000. Some might ask, "What will two or three more trillion dollars in debt really matter?" My answer: "How would you like to be writing a check each month for a ten trillion-dollar mortgage payment?"

3. Increase taxes (payroll or general) to bring in more money to the government.

"How Much Bond Interest Is being Paid?"

Another common question people ask is, "How much is the government paying in interest on the bonds the trust fund holds?"

At present, the combined trust fund assets earned interest paid to bondholders at **an effective annual rate of 5.7 percent.** The interest rate on bonds issued by the government to the trust fund is the same interest rate that other bonds are paying issued on the same date.

According to the 2005 SSA Trustee Report, the Social Security trust fund received $89 billion in earned interest in 2004. How did the trust fund receive payment? What do you think? The federal government just issued more bonds (IOUs) made payable to the trust fund in the amount of $89 billion.

A Fair Argument

Here is my argument (and, I believe, a fair one). The assets in the Social Security Trust Fund are not what many call "hard assets." In other words, you really cannot sell the IOUs, because they are not marketable. The only way money comes back into the trust fund is when

---

FINANCIAL ALERT

What if we had $900 trillion in the Social Security Trust Fund, not just $1.7 trillion? So what? **At some point the federal government will be called upon to pay these funds back. When that time arrives, the question will be, "At what cost to the American people?" Higher taxes? More national debt? Less national defense? Less national security? A national and global financial meltdown?**

the government either raises revenues, cuts other spending, or increases debt (or some combination). The sustainability of the Social Security program cannot be based upon the size of the so-called trust fund.

If the Social Security Trust Fund money *had not* already been spent by the federal government and had been kept *within* the trust fund (the lockbox concept), in the future when the money is really needed, the federal government would not be forced to:

- Reduce federal spending.
- Borrow the money and increase the national debt.
- Increase payroll or general taxes.

Let me ask you, where are the holes in my logic? *Am I missing something here?*

Do you understand my point? ALL DEBT has to be repaid at some point in the future. I don't know how to communicate it more clearly: **The Social Security Trust Fund money has been spent and will need to be repaid by those who spent it,** the federal government—that means you and me.

In order to pay back the money taken out of the trust fund, we will have to cut spending, borrow the money, or raise revenues (taxes).

I rest my case.

But some will still disagree with me on this issue. Well, I will agree with them on one aspect. It is better to have special Treasury bonds (IOUs) sitting in the fund than to have nothing at all! That's the only point I will agree to.

The Federal Budget, the National Debt, and Deficit Spending

As I am sitting here writing, I have to pause and ask myself the question, "Why am I so *adamant* about this point? Why do I have so much passion concerning this issue?"

Good question. In order to understand, I must tell you more about:

- The federal budget
- The national debt
- Deficit spending

Believe it or not, these three are directly related to Social Security and future benefits.

2004 Federal Budget

In the year 2004, the federal government had income of $1.9 trillion, spent $2.3 trillion, and had a deficit of $412 billion. In the same year, the Social Security Trust Fund had income of $657 billion (taxes and interest) and expenses of $501 billion (benefits and administration), for a surplus of $156 billion.

National Debt

As I mentioned earlier, our national debt is over $7.8 trillion. Where did this debt come from? The national debt is a combination of years of (1) our federal government spending more than is coming in—deficits, (2) borrowing from the Social Security Trust Fund, and (3) additional interest accumulating each year on the national debt.

Deficit Spending

When you hear that the federal budget deficit for 2004 was $412 billion, what the government and news media are not telling you is that **the actual deficit was $568 billion, but the government used the $156 billion Social Security surplus to reduce the deficit** to $412 billion.

In other words, the federal government "increased their reported budget revenues by $156 billion," then **spent** the Social Security surplus **this year.**

Oh . . . don't forget that they gave the Social Security Trust Fund a special Treasury bond for $156 billion. That should make you feel better . . .

The Future of the Fund: Dates and Projections

The growing Social Security Trust Fund balance is projected to peak in 2027 before taking a steep dive the next

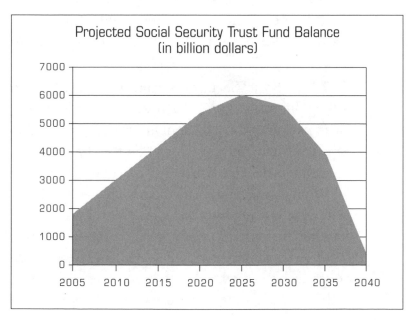

Projected Social Security Trust Fund Balance (in billion dollars)

fourteen years—being fully emptied by 2041. The table "Trust Fund Balances" shows the trust fund balances in 2004 and the future.

TRUST FUND BALANCES
(AMOUNT IN TRUST FUND ACCOUNT)

2004	$1.6 trillion
2018	$3.7 trillion (projected)
2027	$6.6 trillion (projected)
2041	$0 (projected)

I realize that I have already mentioned (in chapter 1) four critical dates regarding the Social Security Trust Fund, but these are the dates everyone needs to remember. Let me summarize.

- **2008:** Cash surpluses in the Social Security Trust Fund will begin to decline. We will still have a surplus each year, but the amount will be less than the year before. In other words, the downward spiral begins in 2008, only three years from now.

- **2017:** The Social Security Administration will begin paying out more money each year than it is collecting in payroll taxes. The annual surpluses since 1983 have vanished, and the annual deficits have begun. This means the Social Security Trust Fund will have to begin using "interest" being received on the bonds each year combined with payroll taxes being collected in order to have enough money to pay promised benefits. Fortunately, enough interest continues to be earned to more than offset the deficit each year, allowing the trust fund assets to grow even further. In other words, payroll taxes and the money earned on bond interest each year still exceed the annual expenses.

- **2027:** The Social Security Trust Fund will need to begin redeeming bonds, in addition to collecting payroll tax revenue and using interest on the bonds, in order to pay promised benefits. Although the trust fund surplus peaks in 2027, a precipitous decline will begin during the year, because tax revenue and interest are no longer able to pay the benefits.

- **2041:** The Social Security Trust Fund will be 100 percent depleted. No more bonds available to cash in, no more interest to be earned. If nothing is done to solve the problem, benefits would need to immediately drop to 74 percent of the promised benefits. (See the chart below.) The trust fund will be depleted, but 74 percent of benefits will still be able to be paid each month. Why? Because payroll

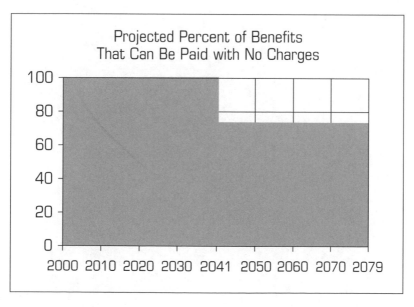

Projected Percent of Benefits That Can Be Paid with No Charges taxes will continue to be deducted from workers' paychecks each month.

OK, enough said about the Social Security Trust Fund. I think you get the picture.

Now it's time for another Social Security review test. Let's see how much you have learned about the Social Security Trust Fund.

1. The 2005 Annual Report of the Board of Trustees of the Old Age &
Survivors Insurance & Disability Income Trust Funds, 5 April 2005, 8.

SOCIAL SECURITY
KNOWLEDGE QUIZ

1. What is a deficit?
   (a) When your expenses exceed your income for the year.
   (b) When your income exceeds your expenses for the year.
   (c) When you cannot pay your debts.
   (d) It's a good thing.

2. What is a surplus?
   (a) When your expenses exceed your income for the year.
   (b) When your income exceeds your expenses for the year.
   (c) When you can pay your debts on time.
   (d) It's really not a good thing.

3. From 1935 to 2005, how many years has the Social Security program had deficit spending?
   (a) None   (c) Every year
   (b) Eleven years   (d) Fifty-five years

4. What is the Social Security Trust Fund balance?
   (a) How much the trust fund owes the federal government.
   (b) The projected Social Security benefits due in the future.
   (c) The cumulative total of all the annual surpluses and deficits, plus the interest earned.
   (d) How much our government owes foreign nations.

5. Every year there is a Social Security surplus, what does the federal government do with it?
   (a) Invest 100 percent in a combination of stocks and bonds.
   (b) Spend 100 percent of it.
   (c) Keep 100 percent in the trust fund.
   (d) Return 100 percent of it to those who paid payroll taxes the same year.

6. What does the federal government give to the trust fund for the money spent?
   (a) An IOU (Special treasury bonds)
   (b) Nothing
   (c) A thank-you note
   (d) Monopoly money

7. In 2004, how much does the federal government owe the trust fund?
   (a) Nothing
   (b) $10 million
   (c) $1.7 trillion
   (d) $270 trillion

8. How will the federal government be able to pay back this debt?
   (a) Decrease federal spending
   (b) Borrow from someone else
   (c) Increase taxes
   (d) One of the above or a combination of all three

9. Where is the trust fund money?
   a) Locked up in a metal filing cabinet in the Social Security office
   (b) Already spent by the government
   (c) In private accounts for future beneficiaries
   (d) No one really knows—it's a secret.

10. When is it projected that the Social Security Trust Fund will be 100 percent depleted (which does not mean that no benefits will be paid)?
   (a) 2010
   (b) 2018
   (c) 2028
   (d) 2041

CHAPTER 5

THE SOLUTIONS

How can we save Social Security?

ACCORDING TO A RECENT *USA Today*/CNN/ Gallup poll, 81 percent of Americans believe "the federal government should make major changes in the Social Security system to ensure its long-term future" in the next one to ten years.[1]

What we need is a long-term solution. In 1983, President Ronald Reagan and Speaker of the House Tip O'Neil offered a proposal intended to solve the problem for the next seventy-five years. Two decades later, Americans are talking about the same problems. Some of the fundamental ingredients must be changed in order to solve the problem permanently! A tax hike, a reduction in benefits, and smoke and mirrors are not going to bring about a permanent solution. All a tax hike or reduction in benefits will accomplish is a postponement of the debate for another few years. We have a moral obligation to solve the problem for generations to come.

Are there solutions to keep Social Security solvent? Absolutely! But the question is, Are we going to continue to use 1935 thinking or 2035 thinking? Times have changed, demographics have changed, financial markets have changed, people have changed—indeed, the world has changed. We would never consider fighting a modern-day war with 1935 equipment. Neither should we consider modern-day financial solutions with 1930s thinking.

According to the 2005 Social Security Trustees Report:

- The cost of doing nothing is an estimated $11.1 trillion.
- If we postpone making changes for just one year, the additional cost will be $700 billion. That amount will increase every year we do nothing.

I am going to approach the potential solutions in the next three chapters. In this chapter I will summarize several options that have been discussed for years. In chapter 6, I will address the plan to partially privatize Social Security by adding private investment accounts. And in chapter 7, I will present my vision for America.

TOP TEN SOLUTIONS

On the following pages I summarize what I believe to be the top ten solutions already being discussed. I have put these solutions in the order of which ones have the greatest potential to solve the problem of insolvency. Let me add that, at the writing of this book, there is no consensus on what should be done. No person or political party wants to be known for being the one to propose increasing taxes, decreasing benefits, or eliminating benefits.

SOLUTION # 1

PROGRESSIVE INDEXING

Presently all initial retirement benefits are based on the increase in average wages (wage inflation) over the forty-five years a person has been working. This calculation is used for everyone, rich and poor. Some have proposed that we limit the use of wage inflation (some call it wage indexing) only to workers who have earned $25,000 or less annually during their working life.

The initial benefits for those who earn between $25,000 and $113,000 annually would be based on a sliding scale using both wage and price inflation. This sliding scale is known as progressive indexing.

Under the proposed progressive indexing, the use of price inflation (some call it price indexing) would be adopted for those who earn $113,000 or more annually.

Historically, wage inflation occurs at a higher rate than price inflation. As a result, the use of progressive indexing would cause benefits for lower-income workers to grow faster than benefits for higher-income workers.

You might be thinking, "Just how much would this change to progressive indexing affect the rich?"

Well, if "progressive indexing" had begun in 1991, here is what the outcome would be today for an individual qualifying for the maximum check being paid in 2004. Under the current system, the retiree would receive $2,111 per month; under progressive indexing, the retiree would be paid $1,587 per month. That's a reduction in benefits of 25 percent, an outcome of the higher-wage earner having his/her benefits calculated based on price inflation. (See the table "Progressive Indexing," page 110, for more information.)

SOLUTION: Progressive Indexing
RESULT: Solves 75 percent of problem for next seventy-five years.

SOLUTION #2

INDEX ALL INITIAL BENEFITS TO PRICES, NOT WAGES

As mentioned earlier, all initial benefits are calculated using "wage inflation," which is historically higher than "price inflation." What if we began calculating *all* initial benefits (for rich and poor) based upon price inflation?

Here is what Alan Greenspan, chairman of the Federal Reserve Board, said about this option: "If the president decelerates increases in benefits by attaching them to prices, not wages, this should eliminate the 75-year projected deficit."

What is the problem with this option? Most point to the long-term problem, not the short term. Wage inflation normally increases 1.5 to 2.0 percentage points more than price inflation each year. Losing 1.5 to 2.0 percent in one year is not a lot, but most point out that over thirty to forty years, this is the equivalent of a 50 percent reduction in benefits.[2]

> **SOLUTION:** Indexing of All Benefits to Prices, Not Wages
> **RESULT:** Solves 100 percent of problem for next seventy-five years.

SOLUTION #3

RAISE PAYROLL TAXES

If we immediately raise the payroll tax for Social Security from 12.4 percent to 14.32 percent, this should stabilize the system for the next seventy-five years.[3]

However, payroll taxes have been increased twenty times since 1935 (see table 4), and the problem still exists! Payroll increases are Band-Aid fixes, not a permanent solution.

If we do nothing until 2041, payroll taxes would have be raised to 16.66 percent and continue to gradually increase to 18.10 percent in 2079.[4] If you don't like 12.4 percent, how much would you like 18 percent?

> **SOLUTION:** Immediate Increase in Payroll Tax from 12.4 Percent to 14.32 Percent
> **RESULT:** Solves 100 percent of problem for next seventy-five years.

SOLUTION #4

CUT BENEFITS

Now, here is another solution that very few people are in favor of—cutting benefits! An immediate reduction in benefits of 12.8 percent would solve the problem for the next seventy-five years.[5]

This would mean that a person presently receiving $950 would begin receiving $828 each month. This could be one option for those under fifty-five years old, but I cannot see this happening to those fifty-five and older. (If we do nothing until 2041— when the trust fund is depleted—the benefits would need to be cut 26 percent to solve the problem, according to the SSA.[6])

SOLUTION: Immediate Cut in Benefits by 12.8 Percent
RESULT: Solves 100 percent of problem for next seventy-five years.

SOLUTION #5

RAISE—OR ELIMINATE— THE SOCIAL SECURITY WAGE CAP BASE

One of the most common solutions you read and hear about is raising the payroll wage cap base to $140,000 or higher.

Some background: In 2005, for every dollar earned in payroll up to $90,000, the employee pays 6.2 percent for Social Security and so does the employer, for a combined total of 12.4 percent. This cap is adjusted each year for inflation. For example, in 2004 the cap was $87,900.

In addition, for every payroll dollar, the employee pays 1.45 percent for Medicare and so does the employer, for a combined total of 2.90 percent. Medicare has no wage cap!

MEDICARE ALERT

Even though Medicare, unlike the Social Security Trust Fund, has no wage cap, it still is struggling with its own funding issues. As challenging as the solution to Social Security might seem to you, let me assure you, the solution is relatively easy compared to what Medicare is going to require. For more information, see the "Medicare Flash" in chapter 1. Why our nation is not addressing the current MEDICARE CRISIS is inexplicable!

The combined Social Security and Medicare taxes total 15.3 percent in 2005.

Let's look at three different illustrations of how this affects the worker's pocketbook:

If you earn $25,000		
	YOU PAY	**EMPLOYER PAYS**
SS at 6.2% each	$1,550.00 ($25,000 X 6.2%)	$1,550.00 ($25,000 X 6.2%)
Medicare 1.45% each	$362.50 ($25,000 X 1.45%)	$362.50 ($25,000 X 1.45%)
If you earn $90,000 (wage cap base for 2005):		
	YOU PAY	**EMPLOYER PAYS**
SS at 6.2% each	$5,580.00 ($90,000 X 6.2%)	$5,580.00 ($90,000 X 6.2%)
Medicare 1.45% each	$1,305.00 ($90,000 X 1.45%)	$1,305.00 ($90,000 X 1.45%)
If you earn $150,000:		
	YOU PAY	**EMPLOYER PAYS**
SS at 6.2% each	$5,580.00 ($90,000 X 6.2%)	$5,580.00 ($90,000 X 6.2%)
Medicare 1.45% each	$2,175.00 ($150,000 X 1.45%)	$2,175.00 ($150,000 X 1.45%)

Even Bill Gates only pays Social Security taxes on the first $90,000 he earns in wages in 2005. (But, like everyone else, he pays Medicare taxes on all his wages!)

Wage Cap for Social Security Payroll Tax
(Earnings up to this amount are subject to SS taxes)

Year Cap Increased	Maximum Taxable Earnings for Year	Year Cap Increased	Maximum Taxable Earnings for Year	Year Cap Increased	Maximum Taxable Earnings for Year	Year Cap Increased	Maximum Taxable Earnings for Year
1937	3,000	1978	17,700	1990	51,300	2002	84,900
1951	3,600	1979	22,900	1991	53,400	2003	87,000
1955	4,200	1980	25,900	1992	55,500	2004	87,900
1959	4,800	1981	29,700	1993	57,600	2005	90,000
1966	6,600	1982	32,400	1994	60,600	2006 P	93,000
1968	7,800	1983	35,700	1995	61,200	2007 P	96,600
1972	9,000	1984	37,800	1996	62,700	2008 P	100,800
1973	10,800	1985	39,600	1997	65,400		
1974	13,200	1986	42,000	1998	68,400		
1975	14,100	1987	43,800	1999	72,600		
1976	15,300	1988	45,000	2000	76,200		
1977	16,500	1989	48,000	2001	80,400		

Source: SSA 2005 Annual Report, p. 124-125.
P = projected

Some supporters of this option appeal to the fact that the net Social Security payroll tax is only 2.23 percent for those earning $250,000 as explained below. I disagree with this opinion, because every worker pays the FULL 6.2 percent for every penny earned up to the cap of $90,000.

Notice how the percent of a worker's payroll tax decreases as he/she earns more than $90,000. If a worker had an annual salary of $140,000, he still pays SS taxes only on earnings up to the annual cap of $90,000; that is, $5,580 in taxes. Therefore, his percentage of SS payroll

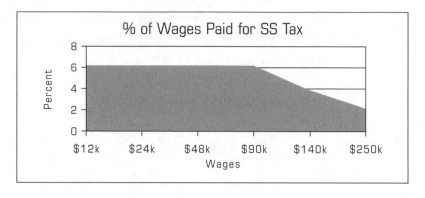

% of Wages Paid for SS Tax

taxes becomes 3.98 percent ($5,580/$140,000=3.98%). A person earning $250,000 will end up paying 2.23 percent of his salary into Social Security ($5,580/$250,000=2.23%).

If we were to raise the wage cap base from $90,000 to $140,000, this additional payroll tax would solve 30 to 40 percent of the long-term problems Social Security is facing, according to projections from the AARP and the *Wall Street Journal.*[7] Raising the wage cap to $140,000 would tax 90 percent of wages, returning to the percentage of wage earnings taxed years ago.

 SOLUTION 5A: Increase of Wage Cap from $90,000 to $140,000
RESULT: Solves 30 percent to 40 percent of problem.

Technically, this would be considered a tax increase, because tax revenues would be increased. Some are opposed to any solution that involves any tax increase. I don't like the fact that it is a tax increase, but this appears to be one solution that would remedy a major portion of the problem.

A more controversial solution is to eliminate the wage cap. In other words, 100 percent of your wages could be taxed for Social Security.

If the cap were eliminated, allowing all wages to be subject to Social Security payroll tax, most project that the Social Security program will be in good shape for the next seventy-five to one hundred years.

SOLUTION 5B: Elimination of Wage Cap
RESULT: Solves 100 percent of problem for seventy-five to one hundred years.

SOLUTION #6

INCREASE ELIGIBILITY AGE

The normal retirement age is slowly increasing from sixty-five to sixty-seven by the year 2027, following congressional legislative approved in 1983. Beginning in 2003, the age for receiving full retirement benefits is increasing by two months per year until it reaches age sixty-six in 2009. The retirement age of sixty-six will freeze from 2010–2020, when it will begin increasing by two months per year until it reaches age sixty-seven in 2027. Notice how the legislation was passed in 1983, but the age increase began twenty years later, in 2003.

Some have proposed that we increase the age of eligibility for full benefits to seventy. By doing this, you would have workers paying into the system for three more years and receiving three less years of benefit payments.

The AARP estimates this solution could solve 36 percent of the problem.[8]

SOLUTION: Raising the Eligibility Age
to Seventy
RESULT: Solves 36 percent of problem.

SOLUTION #7

INVEST A PORTION OF TRUST FUNDS IN INDEXED FUNDS

Why doesn't the Social Security administration invest a portion of the trust fund in stocks and bonds just as corporate America's pension plans do? Some have proposed that we begin to invest a portion, maybe 15 percent, in indexed stock market funds. The long-term results would mean more revenue for the Social Security Trust Fund.

Presently the Social Security Trust Funds are *required by law* to be invested in government bonds. If the trust fund could be invested in stocks and bonds, the government would not be able to spend the surplus each year! How inconvenient for the federal government.

The traditional Social Security system earned an average annual return of 2.9 percent during the past forty years.[9] Most believe the trust fund could do better without taking too much risk, and much of the insolvency problem would be solved just by earning a higher return for the trust fund. But, this would require the trust fund to create a "lockbox" and not let the federal government spend the money each year in return for an IOU.

SOLUTION: A Portion of Fund Invested in Indexed Stock Funds

RESULT: Has potential to solve 15 percent to 45 percent of problem.

SOLUTION #8

TAX ALL OF SOCIAL SECURITY BENEFITS

According to a Social Security brochure, about one-third of people who receive benefits have to pay income tax on their benefits. One proposal is to tax 100 percent of your benefits, no matter what your income.

SOLUTION: Tax on All Social Security Benefits

RESULT: Solves 10 percent of problem.

SOLUTION #9

PRE-FUND SOCIAL SECURITY BENEFITS

If the government immediately put in $4 trillion into the Social Security Trust Fund, combined with future taxes and repayment of $1.7 trillion in bonds, the insolvency would be solved for the next seventy-five years. Of course, funding this amount may be problematic. (See the "cons" in the "Summary of Proposed Solutions" chart.)

SOLUTION: Immediate Infusion of
$4 Trillion to the Trust Fund
RESULT: Solves 100 percent of problem for
seventy-five years.

SOLUTION #10

REPEAL THE PRESIDENT'S TAX CUTS

Some have proposed repealing the federal tax cuts of President Bush. However, this would do nothing to help Social Security. The president's tax cuts did not in any way increase or decrease payroll taxes; nor did they increase or decrease benefits. If the federal income tax reductions were repealed, you could be sure that the federal government would find a way to spend every dollar.

SOLUTION: Repealing of the Federal
Tax Cuts
RESULT: Has no direct effect on Social Security
Trust Fund

THE DO-NOTHING OPTION

Presently, doing nothing seems to be one option. I applaud any person who is putting proposals on the table. We know one thing for sure: Doing nothing is really not an option! If we do nothing today, in 2041 we will be forced into drastic measures such as:

- Raise payroll taxes to 16.66 percent (and continue to raise taxes to 18.1 percent in 2079).
- Cut benefits by 26 percent (and continue to do so until we reach 32 percent in 2079).
- Raise the retirement age.
- Borrow money.
- Raise general taxes.

None of these is an acceptable option.

According to the 2005 SSA trustee report, by not taking action during the twelve months ending in 2004, we added $700 billion in unfunded future Social Security obligations.[10] This amount—$700 billion—will increase every year we postpone action. In other words, our inaction in 2004 cost the SS program $700 billion, and continued inaction in 2005 will cost the system another $700-plus billion—a combined cost of $1.4 trillion for two years of indecisiveness!

If we act soon, small changes could solve the problem!

To Those in the "Growth Camp"

But let me be fair to some who do believe that changes are not required. Some say that the Social Security Administration projections are too pessimistic and that if our economic growth rates continue at the present pace, there is no insolvency problem. Period.

Read what David Walker, comptroller general of the United States, had to say about growing our way out of the problem: "Economic growth can help, but given the size of our projected fiscal gap we will not be able to simply grow our way out of the problem."[11] The comptroller general has told government officials that action on the federal level is necessary.

SUMMARIZING THE TEN SOLUTIONS

Let's summarize the ten possible solutions, this time adding the pros and cons for each proposal:

Summary of Proposed Solutions			
SOLUTION	% SOLVED FOR 75 YEARS	PROS	CONS
1 Progressive Indexing	75%	Helps those who need SS the most—those presently earning $25k or less each year.	Cuts long-term benefits to everyone presently earning $25k or more each year.
2 Index Benefits to Prices, not Wages	100%	More in line with actual inflation.	Reduces benefits long term.
3 Immediately Raise Payroll Taxes from 12.4% to 14.32%	100%	Everyone will be taxed equally.	It's another tax increase!
4 Immediately Cut Benefits 12.8%	100%	Everyone will receive same cut.	Affects poor people who need SS the most.
5 Raise (or Eliminate) Wage Cap from $90k to $140k	30%–40% If eliminate cap 100%	Helps the poor.	Taxes the rich.
6 Increase Age to 70	36%	Helps to account for longer life expectancy.	People will have to work longer.
7 Invest Trust Fund in Stock Market Index Funds	15%–45%	Great potential for higher returns.	Stock market crash.
8 Tax All Benefits	10%	Everyone will be taxed same.	Hurts the poor the most. Takes money out of their pocket.
9 Immediately add $4 Trillion to Trust Fund	100%	Helps fund SS for next 75 years.	Where is the money going to come from?
10 Repeal All Bush Tax Cuts	0%	No direct effect on Social Security Trust Fund.	No direct effect on Social Security Trust Fund.
Do Nothing Option	0%	No increased taxes or decrease in benefits over the short term.	Benefits are guaranteed to decrease to 74% in 2041. Costs $700 billion annually.

Sources: AARP Bulletin, April 2005, 24; www.ssa.gov; and analysis and commentary by author.

In a survey I conducted on the topic of Social Security funding problems, five solutions stood out in the respondents' answers. People were asked, "How would you solve the Social Security problem?" Here is what they said:

- 34 percent—Eliminate or decrease benefits to those who really don't need it.
- 29 percent—Eliminate early retirement age.
- 19 percent—Increase retirement age.
- 13 percent—Increase payroll taxes.
- 5 percent—Decrease benefits.

I was absolutely *shocked* to find that the number one proposed solution by respondents was to eliminate or decrease benefits to those who really don't need it.

You might be thinking, "Well, you failed to mention as one of the solutions the *creation of private accounts*."

Let me explain why. Everyone agrees that the creation of private accounts will not solve the problem of insolvency—in the short term. However, it could play a major role in helping to solve the problem long term. Private accounts could help us move from a pay-as-you-go system to a system where payroll tax money is invested for the worker and the worker receives the benefits of potentially higher returns.

What we don't need is another fix like 1983: raise taxes and cut benefits. This only results in workers paying in more and eventually receiving less.

When are we going to eradicate the philosophy that raising taxes is the solution to our nation's financial problems?

The hardworking citizens of this great nation deserve better solutions than to simply raise taxes and cut benefits. They deserve creative thinking, creative problem solving, and creative proposals.

Before we take an in-depth look at the creation of private accounts in the next chapter, go ahead and complete another Social Security Knowledge Quiz.

1. The poll was conducted 29 April to 1 May 2005, surveying 1,006 adults nationwide; www.pollingreport.com/social.htm

2. *AARP Bulletin,* February 2005, 12.

3. Social Security Administration, "The 2005 Annual Report of the Board of Trustees of the Federal Old-Age & Survivors Insurance & Disability Insurance Trust Funds;" 5 April 2005, 3; www.ssa.gov/OACT/TR/TR05/tN_LRest.html

4. Ibid., 16.

5. Ibid., 3.

6. Ibid., 16

7. Thomas N. Bethell, "What's the Big Idea?" *AARP Bulletin* April 2005, 24, www.aarp.org/bulletin/socialsec/ss_ideas.html; David Wessel, "The Basics of Social Security," *The Wall Street Journal,* 1 February 2005, B4.

8. Bethell, "What's the Big Idea?" *AARP Bulletin,* April 2005.

9. "The 2005 Annual Report of the Board of Trustees," 92.

10. Ibid., 58.

11. Government Accountability Office, "Social Security Reform: Early Action Would Be Prudent;" 9 March 2005, report GAO-05-397T, 16; www. gao.gov/new.items/d05397t.pdf

SOCIAL SECURITY KNOWLEDGE QUIZ

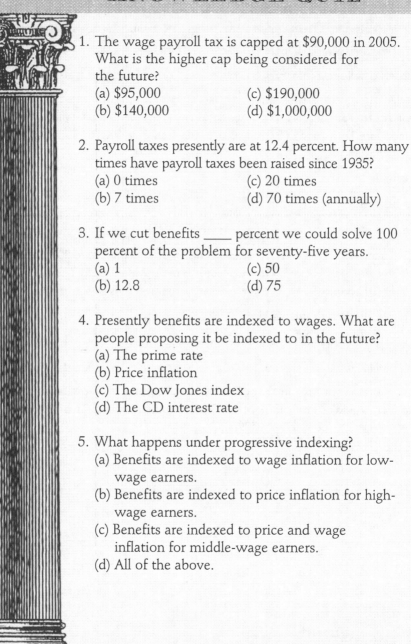

1. The wage payroll tax is capped at $90,000 in 2005. What is the higher cap being considered for the future?
   (a) $95,000   (c) $190,000
   (b) $140,000   (d) $1,000,000

2. Payroll taxes presently are at 12.4 percent. How many times have payroll taxes been raised since 1935?
   (a) 0 times   (c) 20 times
   (b) 7 times   (d) 70 times (annually)

3. If we cut benefits ____ percent we could solve 100 percent of the problem for seventy-five years.
   (a) 1   (c) 50
   (b) 12.8   (d) 75

4. Presently benefits are indexed to wages. What are people proposing it be indexed to in the future?
   (a) The prime rate
   (b) Price inflation
   (c) The Dow Jones index
   (d) The CD interest rate

5. What happens under progressive indexing?
   (a) Benefits are indexed to wage inflation for low-wage earners.
   (b) Benefits are indexed to price inflation for high-wage earners.
   (c) Benefits are indexed to price and wage inflation for middle-wage earners.
   (d) All of the above.

6. What is the normal retirement age for 2027? (This is already the current law.)
   (a) 62   (c) 67
   (b) 65   (d) 70

7. What are some proposing we do with the Social Security Trust Fund surplus?
   (a) Send 100,000 deserving people on a luxury vacation each year.
   (b) Invest a portion in indexed stock funds.
   (c) Buy a gallon of ice cream for everyone on their sixty-fifth birthday.
   (d) Increase benefits for those already over one hundred years old.

8. How will repealing all the recent tax cuts help Social Security?
   (a) It will increase funding for the trust fund.
   (b) It will increase payroll taxes.
   (c) It will not directly help Social Security at all.
   (d) None of the above.

9. What is not an option?
   (a) Do nothing.
   (b) Raise wage base cap to $140,000.
   (c) Raise the retirement age.
   (d) Raise payroll tax.

10. Which of the following options are not being proposed?
    (a) Eliminate the Social Security system—stop paying benefits.
    (b) Invest 100 percent of the Social Security surplus in the stock market each year.
    (c) Stop Social Security payroll taxes for those earning less than $20,000.
    (d) All of the above.

CHAPTER 6

THE PLAN TO PRIVATIZE

Is ownership the best solution?

RECENTLY I WAS THE GUEST on a national radio program, discussing Social Security with the host. During the program, one of the callers asked sarcastically, "How much is President Bush paying you to promote his proposal?" He misunderstood my intent. As I explained on the program, I have no interest in promoting anyone's political agenda, whether it be that of President George W. Bush or former President Bill Clinton. However, I am very interested in promoting something that I believe is good for America.

As I have discussed the topic of Social Security with my family, friends, and groups of all ages, many are surprised to learn that partial privatization of Social Security is not a "recent proposal," but actually has been discussed for many years.

I can only assume that even in 1935 some form of "personalized accounts" was discussed. The pay-as-you-go proposal had to concern President Roosevelt and some members of Congress.

What does it mean to partially privatize Social Security? The partial privatization of Social Security means that workers will be given the opportunity to invest a portion of their Social Security payroll taxes into a private investment account—one they own! At present, 100 percent of payroll taxes goes into the Social Security Trust Fund and is used to pay others' benefits today.

As I see it, **at the heart of partial privatization are three fundamental issues:**

1. The attempt to **change a system** that worked seventy years ago but is unsustainable today. (See chapters 1 and 3 for specific details.) We must begin the transition from a pay-as-you-go system.
2. The attempt to create a sense of **personal responsibility** for each American citizen.
3. The attempt to help singles and families **create real assets** that otherwise they would never own.

Fundamentally, there is nothing wrong with trying to (1) change an outdated program, (2) create greater personal responsibility, and (3) create assets that belong 100 percent to the individual. I believe all three are good for America and can be accomplished by allowing a small portion of the 12.4 percent of Social Security taxes to be invested in private invest-

ment accounts. I am not locked into the current proposed amount of 4 percent; it could be 1 percent or 6.2
percent. Let's not get bogged down in the specifics at
this point. First, a little history of the Social Security
privatization movement.

A Little Privatization History

The 1994-1996 Social Security Advisory Council
proposed three plans, each calling for private investment in financial markets. "The first [plan] called upon
Congress to consider authorizing investment of part of
the Social Security trust funds in equities (on the
assumption that stocks would produce a higher return
to the system). The second would require workers to
contribute an extra 1.6% of pay to personal accounts
to make up for Social Security benefit reductions. . . .
The third would redesign the system by gradually
replacing Social Security benefits with flat-rate benefits based on length of service and personal accounts
(funded with 5 percentage points of the current Social
Security tax rate)."[1]

In 1998 Senator Daniel Patrick Moynihan (D-NY)
wrote a commentary for *U.S. News & World Report*
entitled "How to Preserve the Safety Net: Return to a
'Pay As You Go' System and Allow for Private
Accounts."[2] He explained that some people believe
Social Security is a failed plan, and as a result they
desire to transition Social Security to a system that primarily invests in the stock market—eventually making
everyone a millionaire. He did not believe this was
going to happen, but he did not rule out the possibility that it could happen.

Moynihan and Senator Bob Kerrey (D-Neb.) had introduced legislation in 1998 that would accomplish the following (not all aspects of legislation are listed):

- Cut payroll taxes from 12.4 percent to 10.4 percent immediately.
- Allow individuals to deposit 2 percent of their wages into personal accounts.
- Retain the basic structure of Social Security.
- Move the system back to a true pay-as-you-go system.
- Increase the retirement age to sixty-eight in 2023 and to seventy in 2073.

Early the next year President Bill Clinton introduced a **"1999 reform plan** that would have allocated a portion of any federal budget surplus to personal accounts supplemented by a worker's own contributions and a government match (scaled to income)."[3]

In 2001, President Bush appointed a council to make recommendations to reform Social Security. In its final report (issued on December 21, 2001), the council included three reform options. Like the 1996 Social Security Advisory Council recommendations, each option of the Bush 2001 Social Security Advisory Council recommended some form of voluntary personal account.

Obviously, neither the Moynihan/Kerrey proposed legislation nor the Clinton plan became law. Nor have the recommendations of the two Social Security Advisory Councils (1996 and 2001). In fact, according to the SSA Web site, no major Social Security legislation has been passed since 1996.

A New Proposal to Partially Privatize Social Security

At this writing, President George W. Bush is championing another push to partially privatize Social Security. There is much misunderstanding and confusion about his proposal. Let me try to sort through the maze of miscommunication and summarize the facts.

There is no "official" proposal. Even though I will use the word *proposal*, as of the writing of this book, the president of the United States has not issued his "official" proposal to solve the Social Security problem. However, the president has given many *details* of what his proposal might look like.

What the Proposal Does Not Do

Be sure you check our Web site (www.foundationsfor living.org) for the most recent information on any proposals being offered.

At present, the president is . . .

- *NOT proposing* to totally privatize Social Security. Most people understand this fact, but some do not. It is not his intention to completely dismantle the current system and replace it with an entirely new system.
- *NOT proposing* to change promised benefits to anyone age fifty-five and older. Those who are fifty-five and older are presently depending on the promised benefits or have made plans to be receiving the promised benefits and do not have time to make other plans.

- *NOT proposing* to increase payroll taxes. This could change, but it appears that the president is not open to increasing the 12.4 percent payroll tax.
- *NOT proposing* a temporary fix to Social Security. He desires for the nation to move toward a permanent solution.

SUMMARY OF THE PRESIDENT'S PLAN

Two key ingredients of the Bush plan are benefits and avoiding poverty.

1. *Benefits.* Future generations should receive benefits equal or greater than previous generations.
2. *No Poverty in Retirement.* Social Security should ensure that seniors who have worked hard their entire lives and paid into the system should not have to retire in poverty. The current system does not make this promise.

Two other elements of President Bush's plan are the use of progressive indexing and the option of investing in a personal account.

PROGRESSIVE INDEXING

Progressive indexing is one way to assure that no one will retire in poverty. Under progressive indexing, benefits for lower-income workers would grow faster than benefits for higher-income workers. The benefits for lower-income workers (those who earn less than $25,000 per year) will continue to grow at the rate of

PROGRESSIVE INDEXING

Here is how progressive indexing would affect
those who qualify for the maximum check each month.

Retirement Year	Benefit under Current Plan	Benefit under Proposed Plan
1991	$1,163	$1,144
1992	$1,231	$1,186
1993	$1,289	$1,222
1994	$1,358	$1,254
1995	$1,474	$1,289
1996	$1,501	$1,323
1997	$1,609	$1,361
1998	$1,648	$1,390
1999	$1,684	$1,408
2000	$1,751	$1,443
2001	$1,877	$1,494
2002	$1,988	$1,533
2003	$2,045	$1,554
2004	$2,111	$1,587

Source: "President Touts 'Progressive Indexing' Plan, *USA Today*, 28 April 2005,
www.usatoday.com/news/washington/2005-04-28-bush-ss-plan_x.htm

wage inflation, while those for higher-income workers (those who earn over $113,000 per year) will grow at the rate of price inflation. The initial benefits for those who earn between $25,000 and $113,000 annually will be based on a sliding scale using both wage and price inflation; i.e., progressive indexing. As noted in chapter 5, each year the rate of wage inflation exceeds that of general inflation. Currently initial benefits—for all workers—are calculated on wage inflation, but that would change under the president's plan. This would solve about 75 percent of the problem for the next seventy-five years. The impact of such a plan on retirement benefits is shown on the table on the facing page.

Those age fifty-five and older will in no way be affected by the plan. They will be receiving the benefits as promised, based on current indexing tied solely to wage inflation.

PERSONAL SAVING ACCOUNTS

Here are several of the features of the personal savings account being proposed under President Bush's Social Security plan:[4]

- *Voluntary opt in.* No one will be required to divert any payroll tax money into a private account. The program will be voluntary for those born in 1950 or after. However, once a person decides to begin investing in private account(s), he will not have the choice later to opt out of the plan.

- *Reduction of benefits.* If you choose to invest a portion in a private account, your traditional benefits will be reduced to account for the portion of your fund not going into the traditional Social Security plan.

- *A phase-in period.* Private accounts will not begin to be offered until 2009. Then, they will be phased in over a three-year time frame:

    2009: Those born 1950 to 1965 can enroll.

    2010: Anyone born 1950 to 1978 can enroll.

    2011: Anyone born in 1950 or after can enroll.

- *Maximum 4 percent investment.* Long term, the maximum anyone will be able to invest of their annual retirement contribution would be 4 percent. Beginning in 2009 a person can invest the smaller of either 4 percent of their earnings or $1,000. Thus in 2009 a person earning $50,000 annually can contribute only $1,000 (even though 4 percent of $50,000 is $2,000). Then, the dollar cap will increase by $100 every year. So in 2010, the cap will become $1,100.

- *Investment options.* The current plan calls for investors to have the ability to choose from five investment accounts. Potentially these options could include:

  - U.S. government bonds
  - Conservative mix of stocks and bonds
  - Stock fund index
  - International fund
  - Stock fund

Another option could be some type of a default fund that would be invested at a level of risk according to your age.

- *Management of funds.* The management of funds will not be handled by government, but by private or public companies.
- *No loan option.* You will not be able to request a loan against your private account for any amount.

- *Major decision at age forty-seven.* At age forty-seven, the private fund would automatically be invested into a life-cycle fund for the worker's protection. The life-cycle account would automatically be adjusted each year to reflect the worker's age. The older one becomes, the less investment risk he or she will assume. This will be done to protect the worker from having all his money invested in the stock market and it crashing the month before he retires. (The worker and spouse could sign a waiver to opt out of the default life-cycle fund if they acknowledge they understand the risk involved and are willing to personally assume these risks.)

- *Required purchase of an annuity—if necessary.* If your regular Social Security check would not be enough to keep you out of poverty, you would be required to use all or a portion of your private account to purchase an annuity with a monthly payout for life. This would continue to provide the "safety net" that the government is concerned about any worker losing in the move to privatize, and it would assure that every person has enough money to escape poverty during retirement. Any money remaining in the private account after purchasing an annuity could be left alone, withdrawn monthly, or passed along to heirs.

- *Inheritance.* These private accounts can be bequeathed to survivors. The president said he is concerned about a system that hurts spouses. In the current system, if both the husband and wife are working, and the husband dies before age sixty-two, when the wife retires, she must choose whether she wants to use her plan or her husband's, but she cannot use both. The employee has been working hard all his (or her) life, paying payroll taxes for forty years, yet cannot leave one dollar to the spouse or children. Under the president's plan, your personal savings account can be left to your spouse, and she (or he) may also claim her own account upon retirement.

REAL OWNERSHIP OF YOUR RETIREMENT ACCOUNT

Perhaps the greatest feature promoted under the Bush plan is the real ownership each worker will assume, yielding a significant nest egg even for lower-income workers. According to the White House Web site (www.whitehouse.gov/infocus/social-security/), "A young person who earns an average of $35,000 a year over his or her career would have nearly a quarter million dollars saved in his or her own account upon retirement."

Here are the actual numbers: Of the $35,000, 4 percent invested annually in a personal account equals $1,400 per year. If $1,400 is invested annually in a personal account for forty-five years and earns 5 percent, the account would be worth $223,580. If it only earned 2.5 percent, it would be worth $114,122. And if it earned 7.5 percent, it would be worth $464,890.

What about a person earning $7.00 an hour, working forty hours per week for forty-five years? His annual salary would be $14,560 ($7.00 x 40 = $280 x 52 weeks = $14,560), and by investing 4 percent into a private account, he'd contribute $582 that year. If $582 is invested annually in a personal account for forty-five years (assuming no wage increases each year so that the additional $582 each remains unchanged [highly unlikely]) and earns 5.29 percent, the account would be worth $100,913. If it only earned 2.75 percent, it would be worth $50,578. And if it earned 7.75 percent, it would be worth $208,463.

How excited would a hardworking person earning just over minimum wage all his life be if at age sixty-five he or she had an account with $50,000, $100,000, or $200,000 with his or her name on it? The wage earner could use this account for retirement or, upon death, leave it to a spouse or to his or her kids.

Thus the personal account portion of your Social Security contribution receives compound interest for forty-five years and lets you receive all the benefits. The president believes that wage earners contributing to Social Security should have "hard assets" of their own, and not just a filing cabinet full of IOUs.

THE BASICS OF THE BUSH PLAN

Let's review the basics of the president's plan to offer personal accounts:

- Progressive indexing, except for those age fifty-five and older, whose calculations and benefits remain unchanged
- Voluntary opt in; once in, no later opt out
- Reduction of traditional SS benefits
- Sign-up phased in over three years: 2009–2011

- 4 percent maximum contribution to private account
- Variety of investment options
- No loan option
- Life-cycle account—decision at age forty-seven
- Required purchase of an annuity—if necessary
- Inheritance of account
- Real ownership

Even as good as it looks on paper or charts, the president's plan is not without opposition.

OBJECTIONS TO THE BUSH PLAN

The president's plan is not without controversy—very heated controversy, in fact. Here are what some of his opponents are saying is wrong with his proposal.

OBJECTION # 1

The estimated transitional costs are $1 trillion to $2 trillion (in today's dollars), and this will cause the Social Security Trust Fund to run out of money sooner.

Response: This objection centers on allowing workers to "divert" money that would be going into the Social Security Trust Fund and allowing it to be invested in personal accounts—at a time when the trust fund needs it the most. Therefore, the trust fund depletion date of 2041 would arrive much earlier, due to less money going into the fund. In my opinion this is the best argument against partial privatization and should be debated. So, how do we solve this problem?

I believe the best way to make up the projected transitional costs would be to make "minor adjustments" by a combination of (1) progressive indexing, (2) increasing retire-ment age, (3) keeping the trust fund in a lockbox (not allowing any surplus monies to be withdrawn), and (4) allowing up to 20 percent of the Social Security Trust Fund to be invested in conservative stock and bond investment vehicles. (We discussed several of these approaches in the previous chapter.)

In their 2005 report, the Social Security Board of Trustees estimated the shortfall for the next seventy-five years is $4 trillion (in today's dollars) if we make no changes. Therefore, somehow, some way, by raising payroll taxes, decreasing benefits, or raising general taxes, we will have to make up this $4 trillion shortfall.

Paying $1–$2 trillion for transitional costs sounds much less painful than doing nothing and having to pay $4 trillion and still not helping to solve the long-term problem.

OBJECTION #2

Private accounts do nothing to solve the long-term Social Security deficit.

Response: During the short term, there will be some transitional costs as mention in objection #1; however, during the long term, private accounts could help to solve the problem permanently.

OBJECTION #3

The system has worked great for the past seventy years. Why would we want to change one of the most suc-cessful programs ever created by our government?

Response: Just because something may change does not mean the proposed change will be for the bad. Some changes are very good.

Objection #4

What will happen to senior citizens if the stock market crashes? The president's plan does not offer financial security that can withstand a market-crash scenario.

Response: The president's plan has "safeguards" that help ensure that an individual will not be 100 percent invested in the stock market just before retirement.

Objection #5

Most Americans have very little interest in actively managing their pension plan.

Response: The fact is we live in a different culture than we did seventy or even just thirty years ago. The number of Americans who had any knowledge about an IRA or a 401(k) was very limited back then. Hardly anyone was investing in mutual funds. Very few people actually owned stocks. Today, all of that has changed; familiarity with 401(k) plans and mutual funds, and the level of stock ownership, are much higher.

Objection #6

Allowing personal accounts can result in less benefits being paid.

Response: With private accounts, the possibility of someone receiving less money is very low. However, there is a small risk involved. Which would your rather have: a guaranteed monthly check for $955 every month, or the realistic possibility of receiving double or even triple that amount—and when you die, have something left over to give to your spouse and/or kids?

Objection #7

The administrative costs will be too high.

Response: This is simply not the case. Just examine the administrative cost for the federal employee Thrift Saving Plan (TSP) and company 401(k) plans. The TSP administrative expense is 0.3 percent of assets being managed.

Objection #8

We already have private accounts in the form of investment retirement accounts, or IRAs. Why do we need more private accounts?

Response: IRAs are funded out of your personal checkbook; in contrast, personal accounts will be funded out of payroll taxes already being deducted. This is a *big* difference, letting future retirees use a portion of their Social Security contributions to be personally invested in mutual funds, if they so desire.

It will be very interesting to see how the Social Security debate unfolds in the months—and years—to come. I can only assume that we will be discussing and debating the financial structure well into 2006, if not beyond.

A Common Question

Over the last few months, people have asked me a variety of questions. The most common has been:

"Ethan, what do you believe is the best thing to do?"

Let me explain to you my answer to that question in the next chapter. I have read hundreds of articles on the topic—talked with the young and old, government officials and professional investment advisors.

But, most importantly, I have prayed that God would give me the ability to *understand the issue* and the *wisdom to propose* a workable solution.

It is with this prayer that I offer my analysis in the following chapter.

1. CRS Issue Brief for Congress: "Social Security Reform," IB98048, updated 21 April 2005, 7; http://fpc.state.gov/documents/organization/45974.pdf

2. Daniel P, Moynihan, "How to Preserve the Safety Net," *U.S. News & World Report*, 20 April 1998, 25.

3. CRS Issue Brief for Congress, 7.

4. All years shown under "Voluntary Opt In" and "A Phase-in Period" are based on passage of the plan in 2005. Later legislative approval would alter the years so that anyone age fifty-five and older at the time the legislation is enacted would be exempt from the changes.

SOCIAL SECURITY KNOWLEDGE QUIZ

1. The president's plan will not change any promised benefits for those:
   (a) 55 and older
   (b) 50 and older
   (c) 40 and older
   (d) 25 and older

2. Under the president's plan, the use of private accounts would be:
   (a) Voluntary
   (b) Required

3. Over the long term, what is the maximum amount you would be able to contribute into a private account?
   (a) 1 percent   (c) 4 percent
   (b) 2 percent   (d) 10 percent

4. Once you opt in, can you opt out of private accounts later?
   (a) Yes
   (b) No

5. If you contribute funds into private accounts, your traditional Social Security benefits would:
   (a) Remain the same
   (b) Decrease
   (c) Increase

6. What is the best argument against partial
   privatization of Social Security?
   (a) Everyone will receive less money each month.
   (b) Ownership is not a good thing.
   (c) The transitional cost could be as much as $2 trillion,
       causing the Social Security Trust Fund to run out of
       money sooner.
   (d) None of above.

7. Would you be able to take loans against your private account?
   (a) Yes
   (b) No

8. At what age would your private funds go into a life-cycle
   account—if you do not agree to take personal responsibility
   for investment risk?
   (a) 40
   (b) 47
   (c) 55
   (d) 65

9. If your traditional Social Security benefits will not keep you
   above the poverty level, what must you do?
   (a) Drop out of the system.
   (b) Increase your level of risk.
   (c) Purchase an annuity.
   (d) Quit depending on the government and go out and get
       a job.
   (e) Pray harder.

10. Can your private account be inherited upon your death?
    (a) Yes
    (b) No

CHAPTER 7

THE VISION FOR THE FUTURE

What should our nation's financial priorities be?

OVER THE PAST FEW MONTHS studying the topic of Social Security, I have been reminded first-hand that ignorance is bliss, but knowledge can be painful. The more I study, the more I understand that America is on the wrong course. As I said earlier in the book, America is losing her financial conscience. America is losing her financial alertness. Overspending and mounting debt cannot be sustained long term—even by the United States of America.

Along with hundreds of hours of study, I have sought a deeper perspective with times in prayer, soul searching, and Bible study. One morning while working on this book, I asked God to show me why I should continue spending so much of my time researching and writing about national financial issues. During that time I was struck with the following truths: America has been blessed with resources literally beyond imagination. America has so much potential for good, to do good, and to help fulfill the Great Commission. But unless America regains her financial conscience, we will lose that potential forever. So much God-given potential and so many God-given financial resources will vanish unless we change our course.

During those early morning hours with God, it also became obvious to me that there is a *connection* between America's financial stability and the cause of Christ worldwide. The cause of Christ will be affected globally if America stumbles financially.

Clearly this book is about Social Security, yet we need to consider a greater financial vision for America. Such a vision will help to stabilize programs like Social Security, of course, but it will also put us on a path to long-term financial stability.

Here is my vision—**a fivefold plan to stabilize our nation. For our financial stability, we should:**

1. Honor God as a nation.
2. Balance the federal budget each year.
3. Seek to lower federal income taxes, and do not increase federal taxes.
4. Begin mandatory retirement savings for everyone.
5. Become a debt-free nation and remain debt-free.

Let me briefly explain my position on each of these five goals.

1. HONOR GOD AS A NATION.

Any vision for our nation must begin with God. Beginning in 1963 when our highest court removed prayer from our public schools, American society has worked hard at removing God from the public arena. Prayers using the name of Jesus are scrutinized; manger scenes at Christmas are banned; public displays of crosses are offensive, and the display of the Ten Commandments in public buildings has been outlawed; at times, God's Word is mocked.

God, speaking to the nation of Israel, said,

> Therefore you shall keep the commandments of the Lord your God, to walk in His ways and to fear Him. . . . Otherwise, you may say in your heart, "My power and the strength of my hand made me this wealth." But you shall remember the Lord your God, for it is He who is giving you power to make wealth, that He may confirm His covenant which He swore to your fathers, as it is this day. It shall come about if you ever forget the Lord your God and go after other gods and serve them and worship them, I testify against you today that you will surely perish. (Deuteronomy 8:6,17–19)

The United States has been blessed with great wealth that no other nation has ever known or experienced. The wealth in America is almost incomprehensible compared to other nations. Consider that in just five years (ending in 2004), approximately $10 trillion poured into the U.S. Treasury. *That's a lot of money.*

Why has this nation been so blessed with great wealth?

It is my belief that when our Founding Fathers chartered our nation, they demonstrated a deep faith in God.

It is a documented fact that many had a reverence for God. They honored God.

I can only assume that our Founding Fathers had the same attitude as King David expressed,

> Both riches and honor come from You, and You rule over all, and in Your hand is power and might; and it lies in Your hand to make great and to strengthen everyone. Now therefore, our God, we thank You, and praise Your glorious name. (1 Chronicles 29:12–13)

If we forget God in our schools, our courts, our homes, and our financial institutions, surely we shall perish as a nation. As a nation and as a people, we need to honor God, have a growing respect for God, and never forget God. We need the hand of God and the mercy of God to be upon our nation. Without honoring God as a nation, we as a nation will never be in a position for God to guide, direct, and bless our nation.

2. BALANCE THE BUDGET EACH YEAR.

When you spend more than you take in, you have what is called a deficit. When you take in more than you spend, you have what is called a surplus. In 2004 we experienced the largest deficit to date in the history of the United States: $568 billion. (This includes the amount borrowed from the Social Security Trust Fund.)

Our government spent more than they took in fifty-six of the last sixty-eight years. On average, that's four out of every five years—82 percent of the time! As shown by the following chart, during the last twenty-five years, we have had deficit spending twenty-one times.

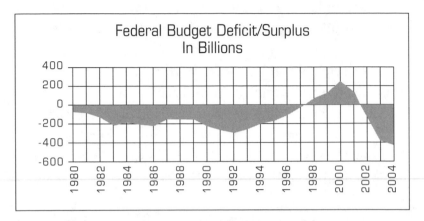

Federal Budget Deficit/Surplus
In Billions

Common sense tells us that our nation needs to balance the budget each year. Living within your means is a fundamental ingredient to financial solvency. Believe it or not, a balanced budget amendment is **not required** for the president and Congress to balance the budget each year. We just need a president and Congress who have the courage to cut unnecessary government spending, and to adopt a **core national value:** living within our means.

For some reason, the federal government believes it does not have to balance the budget each year. They're obviously thinking, "We don't have to spend less than we have in income . . . We're the **United States of America.**"

Significant long-term financial strategies/changes must be put into place beginning immediately. Otherwise, we will spend and borrow our way into destruction. *A nation cannot sustain the amount of debt we are accumulating and survive.*

Whether the president and those serving in Congress want to believe it or not, there will be a point when our federal budget will not be able to bear the strain being placed upon it by Social Security, Medicare, welfare, defense, and repayment of our national debt . . . just to list a few. There is coming a day when the numbers will simply not add up!

In order to balance the budget, we must first focus on entitlement spending (Social Security, Medicare, etc.) and interest on the national debt.

We need to become serious about balancing the federal budget every year—with no exceptions.

FINANCIAL ALERT!

I make very few guarantees, but I am about to make one.
If you consistently spend more than you earn year after year, you will have a financial crisis. This is true for individuals and true for nations.

---

3. SEEK TO LOWER FEDERAL INCOME TAXES, AND DO NOT INCREASE THEM.

Raising taxes is not the solution to our nation's financial problems. As a nation we don't have a revenue problem; *we have a spending problem.* In my research file I have a 1993 letter from a United States senator documenting that since World War II, for every dollar in new taxes raised, Congress has found a way to spend $1.59.[1]

More than forty years ago a Democratic president sounded the call to cut federal taxes. In a 1962 speech, John F. Kennedy said, "An economy hampered by restrictive tax rates will never produce enough revenues to balance our budget, just as it will never produce enough jobs or enough profits. In short, it is a paradoxical truth that tax rates are too high today and tax revenues are too low, and the soundest way to raise the revenues in the long run is to cut the rates now."[2]

I look at it this way. There is a limited supply of money each family has to give, save, spend, and pay taxes. The more money families are *required* to send to Washington, the less money they have to spend for food, cars, vacations, house repairs, investing, and giving.

Our government must find a way to pay the bills and not raise taxes.

4. BEGIN MANDATORY RETIREMENT SAVINGS FOR EVERYONE.

I realize that the discussion about offering private accounts within the Social Security program is very controversial. Even if you strongly disagree, permit me to demonstrate how private accounts could help. I see great merit in some form of mandatory saving for all Americans if they help to create personal ownership. The government has mandatory speed limits, mandatory taxes, mandatory seat belt laws, and mandatory car insurance—all for our good. Why not mandate that all Americans put money into personal investment accounts for their retirement? It will help those who don't have the discipline to invest, and those who have the discipline will applaud it.

Most would agree that the creation of mandatory investment accounts would help to create personal responsibility. We must begin to move away from the mind-set that "it's the government's responsibility" to take care of everyone's needs. Personal responsibility, not entitlements, is what helped to build this great nation. Personal responsibility is what is going to help us survive— with God's help.

Just look what could happen forty-five years from now if workers were allowed to contribute 4 percent of their wages into mandatory personal investment accounts.

Results of Investing 4 Percent of Wages for Forty-five Years			
Return on Investment	$25,000 Wages: 4% Annual Investment = $1,000	$50,000 Wages: 4% Annual Investment = $2,000	$75,000 Wages: 4% Annual Investment = $3,000
2%	$71,892	$143,785	$215,678
4%	$121,029	$242,058	$363,088
6%	$212,743	$425,487	$638,230
8%	$386,505	$773,011	$1,159,516
10%	$718,904	$1,437,809	$2,156,714

Next, let's look at how much you will be able to withdraw annually (for twenty-five years at various rates of return) upon turning age sixty-five. In this illustration, your investment account would be at $0 after twenty-five years.

I should add that in order to have a return on investment of 8 percent or higher, you would need to be willing to assume greater risk. The greater the potential for higher returns also means the greater the potential for loss! Of course, rates of return will vary year to year; even a good mutual fund can lose money in a bad year. Keep in mind that the younger you are, the more risk you can afford to take. The older you become, the less risk you should be taking.

	Amount You Could Withdraw Each Year to Deplete Account in 25 Years		
Return on Investment	If you have $100,000	If you have $500,000	If you have $1,000,000
2%	$5,122	$25,610	$51,220
4%	$6,401	$32,006	$64,012
6%	$7,822	$39,113	$78,226
8%	$9,367	$46,839	$93,679
10%	$11,017	$55,084	$110,168

Another way of managing your investment would be to calculate how much you can withdraw each year and *never use any of the principal.* In other words, how much can you take out for twenty-five (or even thirty-five) years and still have 100 percent of the initial investment available for future use?

	Amount You Could Withdraw Each Year for Any Number of Years and Retain 100 Percent in Investment Account		
Return on Investment	If you have $100,000	If you have $500,000	If you have $1,000,000
2%	$2,000	$10000	$20,000
4%	$4,000	$20,000	$40,000
6%	$6,000	$30,000	$60,000
8%	$8,000	$40,000	$80,000
10%	$10,000	$50,000	$100,000

Now, isn't that interesting? If you have $500,000 in your personal account and can earn a return of 6 percent annually, you—or your spouse or children—will be able to withdraw $30,000 every year forever—without ever touching the principal! I include "your spouse or children" because in most proposals being discussed today, upon your death, your private account balance can be transferred to your spouse or children.

5. BECOME A DEBT-FREE NATION AND REMAIN DEBT-FREE.

Being debt-free should be **another core financial value for our nation!** Many ask, "It is really possible to become a debt-free nation?" Here is another big question I hear people ask: "Would becoming a debt-free nation be good for the economy?"

Alan Greenspan, chairman of the Federal Reserve Board, has served both Democratic and Republican presidents since 1987. The bipartisan chairman and recognized economist has concluded that paying down the national debt is essential to our national health. In 2001 he told financial analysts, "I have long argued that paying down the national debt is beneficial for the economy: It keeps interest rates lower than they otherwise would be and frees savings to finance increases in the capital stock, thereby boosting productivity and real incomes."[3]

A top Democrat on the Senate Finance Committee argues that eliminating the national debt will help our children as much as it helps us. "Reducing the debt helps boost our economy and takes the debt load off our children and grandchildren," Senator Max Baucus (D-Mon.) announced. "If we get to the point where we could actually eliminate the national debt, and then we flinch, we may have squandered a golden opportunity to clear the books for our children and grandchildren."[4]

But is it really possible to pay off the national debt? Well, it was a realistic goal just five years ago! Commenting upon the release of his fiscal 2001 national budget, President Bill Clinton held out hope that the national debt could be retired in a thirteen-year period, based on progress already made. His comments must be taken in context—we had just recorded the nation's largest budget surplus of $237 billion. Everyone was extremely optimistic about the financial future of our nation.

"We're on the way to an achievement that only a few years ago would have been inconceivable, making America debt-free for the first time since Andrew Jackson was President in 1835. . . . Now . . . I [will] attempt to show you what our budget does to the debt, eliminating it by 2013."[5]

Clinton's comments were seen by some opponents as merely propaganda, yet many acknowledge the goal was right, and the possibility existed for eliminating the national debt. However, once more, the national debt begins to grow. Even in early 2000, Clinton acknowledged the challenge: "By the end of this year, we will have paid down the debt by nearly $300 billion. But you can also see [in the chart behind me] that *the debt is still high, far too high"* (emphasis added).[6]

Paying off the national debt would require *unprece-dented* restrained spending on the part of the president and Congress *each and every year.* One aspect of a balanced budget would be to allocate a portion of the budget to reduce (not add to) the national debt each year. Once we are 100 percent debt-free, just think how we will be able to use the billions of dollars being freed up each year! (See "A Look into a Debt-Free Future" on page 138 for more on this exciting concept.)

Did you realize that in 2004 our government paid more than $322 billion in interest on the national debt? That's almost $1 billion a day we are paying in interest. In the past five years (ending in 2004), our nation has paid $1.7 trillion in interest. That's $1,700,000,000,000 in interest in five years.

$8,000,000,000,000

The number above represents the approximate amount of our national debt. It is my opinion that our growing national debt is going to threaten our nation's financial security and, unless controlled, will be detrimental to programs such as Social Security.[7]

Let's take a quick look at our nation's debt over the past twenty-five years. It took our nation more than two hundred years (1778 till 1980) to reach the level of $1 trillion in national debt. In just twenty-five years we increased our debt to $7.8 trillion.

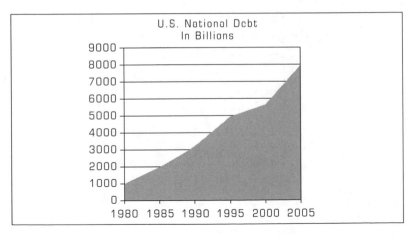

U.S. National Debt
In Billions

This twenty-five-year period represents an average debt growth-rate of 8.9 percent per year. You might be wondering whether that is in line with recent years. Well, on September 30, 2003, our debt was $6.78 trillion, and on September 30, 2004, the national debt was $7.38 trillion. That was a one-year increase of 8.85 percent.

If we use our average growth rate of 8.9 percent (which should be an acceptable figure to use), our national debt will become:

# Yrs	Year	Debt in Trillions
5	2010	$12.0
10	2015	$18.4
15	2020	$28.2
20	2025	$43.1

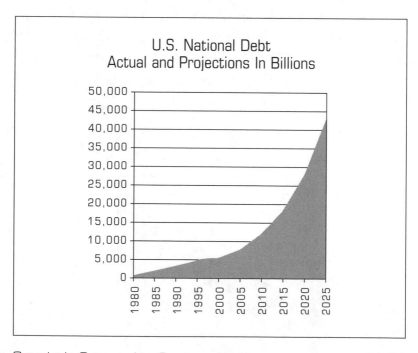

U.S. National Debt
Actual and Projections In Billions

Perhaps you don't like my projections using the actual average growth rate of 8.9 percent. You think it's unrealistic. Well, I disagree, but let's recalculate using a much more conservative 5 percent annual growth:

# Yrs	Year	Debt in Trillions
5	2010	$10.0
10	2015	$12.8
15	2020	$16.3
20	2025	$20.8

If we only had to pay interest of 5 percent (which is low), just look at how much our nation would be paying in interest:

Year	Debt in Trillions	Annual Interest (Billions)	Monthly Interest (Billions)	Daily Interest (Billions)
2010	$10.0	$500	$42	$1.39
2015	$12.8	$640	$53	$1.77
2020	$16.3	$815	$68	$2.27
2025	$20.8	$1040	$86	$2.88

As you can see, interest at 5 percent on $20.8 trillion is $1.04 trillion every year. That's one trillion, forty billion dollars every year, or almost three billion dollars every day—and that's just the interest!

As I have documented above (see President Clinton's comments), only five years ago we were looking at the realistic possibility of becoming debt-free! We need to seize the opportunity before it becomes too late.

A Look into a Debt-Free Future

Look into the future with me. After we pay off our national debt, look at what could happen if our nation began "investing" the money we had been using to pay interest and principal. What if the billion dollars a day (well, almost a billion) that we are currently spending in interest on the national debt could be used to . . .

- Create a national endowment
- Lower or eliminate Social Security payroll taxes
- Lower or eliminate federal income taxes
- Increase funding for medical research
- Increase scientific research
- Increase funding for education
- Increase funding for job training
- Increase funding for new roads and transportation systems
- Increase funding for international humanitarian aid
- Increase funding for national parks and wildlife
- Provide new jobs

The potential for lower taxes and increased funding is absolutely astonishing if you are on the lending side of interest, and not on the paying side.
What if our nation became debt-free and we had the financial resources to begin investing $500 billion per year and average a return of 5 percent on our investment? As the chart below shows, the return on investment would exceed one-half *trillion* dollars in just fifteen years. Our government could make loans to developing nations,

loans to first-time homeowners or small businesses. In effect, we could create a national endowment.

Income from a National Endowment Fund		
Years	Value of National Endowment	Potential Annual Income at 5%
5	$2.8 trillion	$140 billion
10	$6.3 trillion	$315 billion
15	$10.8 trillion	$540 billion
20	$16.5 trillion	$825 billion
25	$23.9 trillion	$1.2 trillion
30	$33.2 trillion	$1.7 trillion

How could this annual income from the national endowment be used? I could come up with a hundred different ways, but imagine if the federal government chose to use the annual income to lower federal income taxes.

Think with me. Could it be possible in fifty or one hundred years that our taxes could be reduced or totally eliminated? Can you imagine what it would be like to no longer have to pay any income tax? We wouldn't need to collect taxes from our citizens, because the national endowment would be creating enough income to partially or fully cover our federal budget. You say impossible? Let me ask you this question: If it's impossible, why are there states that do not have to charge their residents state income taxes? It's because they have enough resources coming in without a state income tax. If it can work for states, it can work for the federal government.

Let's become a debt-free nation!

There you have it, my five-point proposal to help **financially stabilize our nation:**

- Honor God as a nation.
- Balance the federal budget each year.
- Seek to lower federal income taxes, and do not increase them.
- Begin mandatory savings for everyone.
- Become a debt free nation.

Maybe it's not a perfect plan, but I am confident it would head America in the right direction. *Let me know what you think.*

1. Letter from Senator Jesse Helms to Ethan Pope, 16 March 1993.

2. *Financial Planning,* March 1996, 31.

3. Alan Greenspan, "The Paydown of Federal Debt," speech to the Bond Market Association (via videoconference), White Sulphur Springs, West Virginia, 27 April, 2001.

4. "Baucus Explores Ways to Cut National Debt, Provide for Large Tax Cut and Other National Priorities," Press release, office of Senator Max Baucus, 29 March 2001; http://www.baucus.senate.gov/~baucus/Press/01/03/2001424834.html

5. "Remarks by the President at Release of Fiscal Year 2001 Budget," Presidential Hall, 7 February 2000; http: usembassy-australia.state.gov/ hyper/2000/0207/epf103.htm

6. Ibid.

7. Consider the promise and warning regarding debt the Lord gave the nation of Israel in Deuteronomy 28:12–13. Later, in verse 44, the Lord warns of the curse of debt.

1. Is a balanced budget amendment required for our nation to pass a balanced budget?
   (a) Yes
   (b) No

2. Approximately how much is our national debt?
   (a) $8 billion
   (b) $800 billion
   (c) $8 trillion
   (d) $800 trillion

3. During the last sixty-eight years, how many years has our government run on a deficit?
   (a) 68 of 68 years
   (b) 56 of 68 years
   (c) 4 of 68 years
   (d) What's a deficit?

4. If a person earns $50,000 a year and invests 4 percent of it in a private account, and it earns 6 percent for forty-five years, how much would it be worth?
   (a) $222,867
   (b) $334,301
   (c) $111,433
   (d) $425,487

5. If a person has $500,000 in a private account and it is earning 6 percent, how much could that person take out of the account annually for twenty-five years (and fund would be depleted)?
   (a) $10,000
   (b) $39,113
   (c) $78,726
   (d) $5,122

6. If a person has $500,000 in a private account that is earning 6 percent annual interest during his retirement years, how much could that person take out of the account annually (forever) and still retain 100 percent of the principle?
   (a) $10,000   (c) $50,000
   (b) $30,000   (d) $6,000

7. What does our nation need to develop?
   (a) Vision that can look fifty to one hundred years into the future
   (b) A strategy to raise taxes
   (c) A strategy to waste more money
   (d) More schedules for the 1040 tax return

8. What could potentially be two benefits of a national endowment?
   (a) Lower or eliminate federal taxes
   (b) Lower or eliminate Social Security taxes
   (c) Both a & b
   (d) You're dreaming—none of the above.

9. If we paid off the national debt and began investing/loaning $500 billion a year, how much would our national endowment be worth in twenty years?
   (a) $1 trillion   (c) $16.5 trillion
   (b) $6.5 trillion   (d) $165 trillion

10. What is a primary goal of the author's five-part plan?
   (a) Help financially secure our nation long term
   (b) Help people take more luxury vacations
   (c) Help more Americans live in bigger homes
   (d) Help more Americans be able to eat more ice cream

CHAPTER 8

THE BIBLICAL
RESPONSE

What should we be doing as believers?

IN RESPONSE TO THE FIRST seven chapters, several penetrating questions come to mind that we must answer as a nation and individually:

- Are we being good stewards over the resources God has entrusted to us? (Psalm 24:1)
- Are we looking to God for wisdom and direction? (Proverbs 3:5–6)
- Are we honoring God with our wealth? (Proverbs 3:9–10)
- Does our nation have too much debt?
- As a nation, are we financially headed in the right direction?
- Do we attribute our wealth and power to God? (Deuteronomy 8:17–19)
- Do we honor God? (Titus 1:16)

The Philosophical Question

At the very core of the Social Security debate is a philosophical question.

Does our nation have the responsibility to provide a minimal level of income (safety net) for all our citizens in their senior years?

How we answer that question seems crucial to understanding this country's proper roles as caregivers to its older citizens in need. So, let me answer that question by making several observations.

To answer the key question of whether this country should provide a minimal level of income for all our citizens in their senior years, here are six observations:

- Throughout Scripture, we see that God is deeply concerned about the widows, the orphans, and the poor.[1] "The righteous is concerned for the rights of the poor, the wicked does not understand such concern" (Proverbs 29:7). What concerns God should concern us as a nation.

- To whom much is given, much shall be required (see Luke 12:48). If any nation has been a recipient of the blessing of God, our nation has. God will hold our leaders and us accountable for how we dispersed the trillions and trillions of dollars He entrusted into our stewardship.

- However, we are also directed to be good stewards over the personal resources entrusted to us. We are not to waste, but to carefully manage (Luke 16).

- We must not allow entitlements (Social Security, Medicare, Medicaid, welfare, etc.) to get out of control, or they will financially destroy our nation. Some projections are showing that entitlements could be consuming 75 percent of the federal budget in 2050, unless changes are made. If we allow entitlements to overtake our budget, everyone loses: our nation, the world, the cause of Christ, and everyone receiving entitlements. *We must not destroy the tree that is producing the fruit.*

- With a handful of exceptions, churches have not fulfilled their God-given responsibility to care for the poor, the widows, the orphans, and the financially needy. I would estimate there are less than one hundred churches in the nation who disperse more than 10 percent of their annual budget to help those in financial need. I understand the challenges involved. We don't want to be a dispenser of money just because people show up at our door. Good programs require an investment of staff and ongoing accountability. I have not done my part in this area to help, so I am not casting any stones. But we all know that if the church were to operate as God intended, many of our government programs could be eliminated.

- Until that day becomes a reality when American churches support the widows, orphans, and financially needy as God has intended, I believe our nation has an obligation, *a moral responsibility,* to be sure that our citizens are able to live their senior years with basic needs provided.

Beyond our moral responsibility to help sustain our senior citizens during their retirement years, we also need to prepare our youth to become financially responsible. Teaching personal financial responsibility should occur in our schools, churches, and homes. How do young people learn to become responsible unless someone teaches them? I wonder how many people reading this book were required to take a personal finance class while in high school or college. I would be shocked if it were more than 10 percent. Who is teaching young adults to be smart money managers?

With such a poor financial education system, why are we shocked when we read that 22 percent of those over sixty-five years depend on Social Security for 100 percent of their income? Money management must become a part of our core curriculum in schools.

BEING ACTIVE PARTICIPANTS

Whether it be Social Security, the national debt, or balancing the federal budget, God has not called Christians to be passive in government affairs, but to be active. Jesus said that we should be lights shining on the hill—for the cause of Christ. We need to let our light shine, and shine brightly. The more lights that stand on the hill and shine together, the brighter the light and the farther away it can be seen. I don't want hard times to come upon our nation. But, greater than that, I don't want to lose our potential to advance the cause of Christ in our communities, in our states, in our nation, and around the world. Don't miss the connection between the financial stability of our nation and the cause of Christ.

- Get involved. Let your voice be heard. Let your light be seen (see Matthew 5:16).

- If you think the federal government should not be spending the Social Security Trust Fund surplus—tell them. Equally so, if you think it's acceptable—tell them to keep up the good work!

- If you think the federal budget should be balanced—tell them. Let your light shine. If you think it's acceptable to spend more than you earn—tell them to go out and borrow several trillion dollars more!

- If you think the national debt is excessive—let your voice be heard.

As you can see below, the United States has been blessed with wealth beyond compare with other nations. Here are a couple more statistics:

- In 1996, 4.9 million households in the United States each had a net worth of $1 million (not counting their homes), *Money* magazine reported. By 2004 that number had grown to 8.2 million.[2] This number is projected to become 12.5 million in 2009 (52 percent growth), just five years later.

- In 1996 there were 250,000 households with $5 million in net worth. In 2004 that number had expanded to 720,000.[3]

Yet with these blessings comes responsibility. You might be thinking, "If America has so much wealth, why should we be concerned about our financial future?" Good question. Present wealth does not guarantee a secure financial future. The financial instability that looms should compel us to action as a nation and as individuals to be good stewards over the resources God has entrusted us. As Christians, we must let our lights shine by promoting good personal and national stewardship.

How to "Let Your Light Shine"

Here is a list of practical ways you can let your light shine.

- Pray daily for our nation and leaders.
- Elect those who represent your values—ask questions.
- Write your government officials.
- Phone your government officials.
- Personally visit your government officials.
- Send e-mails.
- Organize petitions.
- Write letters to the editor.
- Write news releases.

God has called each of us to be responsible stewards and citizens. It is amazing what one person can accomplish if he or she has the willingness to be persistent and desires to bring about change.

In the next chapter I will be showing how you can **take personal responsibility** for your retirement needs, **regardless** of what the government provides for you.

NOTES
. . . .

1. See Exodus 22:22; Leviticus 19:9–10; Proverbs 14:21–31; 17:5; 19:17; 21:13; 22:22; 29:7; Jeremiah 5:26–29; 7:6; 22:3; 1 Timothy 5:8; James 2:15–16.

2. *Money,* May 2005, 100.

3. Ibid.

CHAPTER 9

PERSONAL PREPARATION

What should you be doing to prepare for the future?

YOU MIGHT BE ASKING at this point, "What are the solutions?" Let me answer that question by shifting the focus of this book from the government and what they are doing right and wrong . . . to you.

What are you doing right or wrong?

You're saying, "I was somewhat enjoying this book until you began shifting the focus to me."

Well, the truth is you cannot control Congress and the president. But you **can control your personal budget, your personal retirement fund, and your personal goals. I encourage you to create your own retirement fund.**

I believe that every American should take personal responsibility for his or her retirement plan. If more people did just that, the government would not be required to tax workers and turn around and distribute the revenues to senior citizens. It is very possible that our Social Security program would only need 20 percent of its present revenue to take care of the nation's needy. Carefully think about these two statements:

Most people will earn in excess of one million dollars during their working life.

Most people will consume practically 100 percent of their income during their working life.

Do you realize, if you earned an average of only $23,000 each year during your working life, more than one million dollars would pass through your checking account? Most will earn far more than one million dollars during their life. Assuming a working career of forty-five years, here's how different salaries would affect one's total earnings:

Annual Earnings	Total Earnings
$23,000	$1,035,000
$46,000	$2,070,000
$100,000	$4,500,000

At the end of your life, how much will you have wasted? How much will you have saved? How much will you have given? On the following pages I will offer specific direction on how **you** can establish and implement a plan for **your** future. These "preparation pointers" will help you grow your personal retirement fund.

First, I recommend you sit down and write your goals on paper.

Jesus said, "For which one of you, when he wants to build a tower, does not first sit down and calculate the cost to see if he has enough to complete it?" (Luke 14:28). I understand the intent of this verse and the surrounding verses is to teach us about counting the cost of discipleship. Good disciples look ahead, calculate the cost, and make wise decisions.

What is the first thing this verse says we need to do? Sit down. Now, I find that somewhat strange. If I have a task to complete, I want to work on it—now! But the absolute best thing I can do is sit down and plan, and I can only assume that prayer would be an important aspect of my initial planning.

My surveys reveal that only 10 percent of people have ever taken the time to sit down and establish written goals.

Proverbs 21:5 says, "The plans of the diligent lead surely to advantage, but everyone who is hasty comes surely to poverty." I look at it this way:

PLANS + DILIGENCE = ADVANTAGE

Just look at some sobering statistics:

- One of five Americans age sixty-five and older (22 percent) depend entirely on Social Security for their retirement income.[1]

- One of three Americans over age sixty-five (33 percent) depend on Social Security for up to 90 percent of their income.[2]

- Two of three Americans over age sixty-five (66 percent) depend on Social Security for 50 percent or more of their income.[3]

- Seven of every ten retirees (70 percent) say they wish they had saved more during their working years.[4]

- It is estimated that as many as 25 million boomers have little or nothing set aside for their senior years. This represents about one-third of boomers.[5]

I make very few guarantees in life, but I feel certain about the following prediction: If you don't establish a plan to save and invest during your working life, you will be in the group that is 100 percent dependent on the federal government for every dollar they receive each month.

MY ADVICE: Finish reading the rest of this book, sit down with a glass of milk and some homemade cookies, and ESTABLISH YOUR GOALS!

2. SAVE 10 PERCENT, EARN 8.5 PERCENT

Goals don't have to be complicated. In my opinion, the simpler the better!

Let me begin by giving you a simple goal that I developed several years ago when I was writing my first book,

How to Be a Smart Money Manager. I was sitting at my desk trying to create an illustration for the chapter on setting goals. Then all of a sudden, the details for "Save 10 Percent, Earn 8.5 Percent" began to fall into place. I could hardly believe it was possible the first time I calculated the numbers.

What would happen if young adults who just finished high school or college decided to faithfully save 10 percent of their wages every paycheck and averaged an annual return of 8.5 percent . . . and did this for forty-five years?

Know what would happen? They would have an investment account at age sixty-five equal to slightly more than **100 percent of the money they earned during their entire working lives!**

Sound impossible? It might be easier than you think!

Take a look at the following chart from *How to Be a Smart Money Manager.*[6]

(1)	(2)	(3)	(4)	(5)
Annual Earnings	Total Earnings After 45 Years	Save 10% Each Year during 45 Years	Total Saved	Total Worth of Fund
$25,000	$1,125,000	$2,500	$112,500	$1,126,325
50,000	2,250,000	5,000	225,000	2,252,651
75,000	3,375,000	7,500	337,500	3,378,977
100,000	4,500,000	10,000	450,000	4,505,303

Column 2 = Annual earnings (1) X 45 years

Column 3 = Annual earnings (1) X 10 percent

Column 4 = 10 percent savings each year (3) X 45 years

Column 5 = Total worth of annual savings (3) earning 8.5 percent each year

Look at this amazing analysis again. If you save 10 percent of your wages every year, earn 8.5 percent, and do this for forty-five years, you will have an investment account equal to every dollar you ever earned!

It's like you worked for forty-five years and at age sixty-five have an investment account equal to every penny you ever earned during your working life. In other words, it would be like you had been receiving two paychecks every payday. Every time you earned $1,000 in wages, you received a $1,000 check and $1,000 was **put away for your future use.**

The best is yet to come!

I know this sounds too good to be true, but it even gets better. Not only would you have every dollar you ever earned, but if your investment keeps earning 8.5 percent, at age sixty-five, you could begin to withdraw approximately four times your average annual salary. This could go on forever, and you would always have 100 percent of your lifetime earnings in the investment account.

Imagine:

**Withdraw four times your average
annual earnings each year—forever!**

How can this be? This is the power of compounding—reinvesting the investment return and leaving the principal untouched—and it requires only that you (1) start early, (2) invest year after year, and (3) continue for the long term (in this case, forty-five years). Let's assume you have been earning at least $25,000 each year during your working life. Since age twenty you have been saving 10 percent—$2,500—every year for forty-five years and earned an average 8.5 percent each year. Here's the result: By age sixty-five, your investment account is now worth $1,126,325! You are able to withdraw $95,737 ($1,126,325 x 8.5% = $95,737) every year forever . . . and still have your investment account of $1,126,325 at age ninety-five!

Now, you will have to agree this suggested goal is simple, achievable, and has great rewards!

MY ADVICE: If you are young, and establish no other financial goals . . . *DO THIS ONE!* Start saving now—not at age thirty-five or fifty—and take advantage of the principle of compounding your investment returns.

3. ENGAGE IN A STEADY INVESTING PROGRAM

Have you tried the steady, plodding investing program? Proverbs 21:5 says, "Steady plodding brings prosperity" (TLB). I like that! Steady, consistent, systematic, methodical investing brings prosperity. That's the principle behind the save 10 percent, earn 8.5 percent program.

Now let's apply it to specific retirement programs available to you. The following charts show what can be accomplished with a systematic investment program, such as a 401(k), 403(b), or personal investment program. Even when investing less than $2,500 per year (see the $50-per-month and $100-per-month charts), the returns become significant when reinvested for the longer term.

No wonder when asked what one of his greatest discoveries was, Albert Einstein replied it was compounding interest.

If You Invest $50 per Month with Various Rates of Return

	6%	8%	10%	12%
10 Years	8,194	9,147	10,242	11,501
20 Years	23,102	29,451	37,968	49,462
30 Years	50,225	74,518	113,024	174,748
40 Years	99,574	174,550	316,203	588,239

If You Invest $100 per Month with Various Rates of Return

	6%	8%	10%	12%
10 Years	16,388	18,294	20,484	23,003
20 Years	46,204	58,902	75,936	98,926
30 Years	100,451	149,036	226,048	349,496
40 Years	199,149	349,100	632,407	1,176,477

If You Invest $250 per Month with Various Rates of Return

	6%	8%	10%	12%
10 Years	40,969	45,736	51,211	57,509
20 Years	115,510	147,255	189,842	247,313
30 Years	251,128	372,589	565,121	873,741
40 Years	497,872	872,751	1,581,019	2,941,193

If You Invest $500 per Month with Various Rates of Return

	6%	8%	10%	12%
10 Years	81,939	91,473	102,422	115,019
20 Years	231,020	294,510	379,684	494,627
30 Years	502,257	745,179	1,130,243	1,747,482
40 Years	995,745	1,745,503	3,162,039	5,882,386

MY ADVICE: Begin doing something this month. It's best to begin early, but even if you have only ten years before you turn sixty-five, begin a steady investing program.

4. DON'T DEPEND 100 PERCENT ON THE FEDERAL GOVERNMENT

As I documented earlier in the book, 22 percent of those over age sixty-five are 100 percent dependent on the government for income.

Now, this brings up an interesting question for you to consider. Is it more honoring to God to spend every dollar you earn during your working life and be dependent upon the government when you retire; or would it be more honoring to God to save a small portion (5 percent or 10 percent) of your earnings each month and be able to meet most, if not all, of your financial needs later in life?

I think the latter honors God more.

Let's begin to lift the burden off the federal government in the area of Social Security and welfare.

MY ADVICE: Don't be 100 percent dependent on the government.

5. BECOME DEBT-FREE

Another important part of your plan will be to become 100 percent debt-free. Yes, that even includes your home.

Most Americans have the attitude, "I will have debt until I die." Well, we need to change that attitude and have people begin thinking, "It's going to be great when I am debt-free" or "It's awesome to be debt-free!"

I remember the day that Janet and I became debt-free . . . December 6, 1988. How did we do it? All I can say is it was a lot of hard work and a willingness to move to a smaller house and a different neighborhood.

We had been married for six years and had been prepaying on our mortgage and building up sweat equity. Just in case you don't know what sweat equity is, it's when (1) you paint the house, (2) you put up the wallpaper, (3) you put in the kitchen faucet, (4) you replace the shower door, (5) you landscape the yard, (6) you repair the wall, and (7) you install the kitchen counter.

We sold our house and purchased a home valued at 46 percent of the one we had just sold. Perhaps you are thinking, *Ethan and Janet probably lived in a luxury house and sold it to purchase an above-average house.* I will let you be the judge: We sold our house for $150,000 and purchased our debt-free house for $69,800. Yes, we have moved since we purchased our debt-free home back in 1988, and today our home remains debt-free.

I am not saying that everyone needs to do what Janet and I did. But I am challenging you to establish your plan to pay off your mortgage as soon as possible.

If you can become free of debt earlier in life—fantastic. But at least establish a schedule so you will have your mortgage paid in full a year or two before you retire. Think how much your financial picture will improve when you don't have any more mortgage payments!

MY ADVICE: Become debt-free!

6. USE A MAP

More than twenty years ago I designed a budgeting system called MAP. That stands for the Money Allocation Plan. It's a simple system that operates on one piece of paper each month. (Well, it is one piece of paper, but it's 11 by 17 inches in size, which folded in half is only 8.5 by 11.) I am convinced that every family needs to use either my MAP system or some type of budget system.

A MAP helps you to maximize the resources God has entrusted to you. Here's how it works: When you receive a paycheck, you "allocate" money (using the MAP form) into what I call MAP money boxes such as *giving, food, transportation,* and *clothing.* When you spend money out of your checkbook, you simply subtract money "out of" the proper category. For example, let's say you allocated $300 into your *food* MAP money box. The next day you write a check for $100 to purchase food. Later that day, or at the end of the week, you would subtract $100 from your *food* MAP money box, showing that you have $200 remaining to spend for food for the rest of the month. It's just a very simple way to keep track of your spending.

What are the benefits of mapping? Here are six:

- Direction
- Maximize resources
- Less waste
- Less stress
- Fewer family fights
- Simple (one page)

It also allows you to accomplish three things:

- Generosity in your giving
- Consistency in your giving
- Freedom in your spending

I like to tell married couples that a MAP will help them have "more fun and less fights!"

Several years ago I wrote a book explaining how to use my simple, one-page MAP system: *Creating Your Personal Money MAP.* For more information, see my Web site, www.foundationsforliving.org. (Click on the resource link and look for the MAP Pack Special [which includes Creating Your Personal Money MAP book, a one-year supply of forms, and an instructional CD].) I receive letters from MAP users on a regular basis. Just the other day Stu wrote and said, "Using the MAP we always have money in our account, which helps remove a lot of stress. We don't see how we ever lived without them. Thanks."

MY ADVICE: Give the MAP system a test drive. Create your personal money map.

7. CREATE AN
INCOME PRODUCING ASSET

Now, preparation pointer 7 is not for everyone; but if you have the personality for it, it's great. You might be thinking, "What could he be talking about?" I'm referring to ownership of rental property.

During your retirement years, how great would it be if your home was debt-free, but you also owned another home that was debt-free, and every month someone sent you a check in the mail? What if you were able to own two or three rental properties?

Back in 1997 Janet and I purchased a rental property. It has been leased out practically every month since that time. We put it on a fifteen-year mortgage, and it will be paid for in 2012.

You might be saying, "Ethan, I thought you just told me to become 100 percent debt-free?" You're right, I did! The focus of that aspect of your plan was your personal home! I believe it needs to become debt-free as soon as you can make it happen.

I do not see a problem with purchasing rental property as long as you . . .

- have prayed about your decision;
- are in agreement with your spouse;
- understand the risks and benefits—as well as headaches;
- keep your personal home debt-free;
- obtain a fifteen-year (or less) mortgage;
- will not need to use the surplus income each month for personal living expenses;
- make sure rental property value of the home far exceeds the mortgage;
- have adequate money in savings to pay for repairs;
- have adequate money in savings to pay the mortgage if it sits vacant for a few months;

- pay your credit card bills in full each month;
- live on a MAP or budget; and
- are willing to invest some of your personal time in your investment.

FINANCIAL WARNING!

Let me SHOUT the following warning using my financial megaphone: **If you are not doing the things listed above, *don't* purchase rental property!** You will only create more problems and massive financial stress for yourself and your family.

Don't ignore the above warning. However, if you qualify and are able to buy an income-producing property . . . and are willing to put up with a few headaches for fifteen years . . .

- you will own another home debt free.
- its value will appreciate every year (in most cases).
- it will be producing income every month for the rest of your life.
- it could be producing income for your children in the future—for many years.

Again, this suggestion is not for everyone, but it just might be a good one for you.

MY ADVICE: Check into purchasing RENTAL PROPERTY.

8. BEGIN RETIREMENT PLANNING TODAY

The sooner you begin planning for retirement the better. Even if you are fifty-five years old, it is not too late to begin. Doing something for the next ten years is better than doing nothing for the next ten years.

Examine the following table and chart to see why it is so important to begin as soon as possible!

Goal: $100,000 at Age Sixty-five Amount You Need to Invest Each Year				
Rate of Return	Age 25	Age 35	Age 45	Age 55
4%	$1,052	$1,783	$3,358	$8,329
6%	$646	$1,264	$2,718	$7,586
8%	$386	$883	$2,185	$6,902
10%	$225	$607	$1,745	$6,274

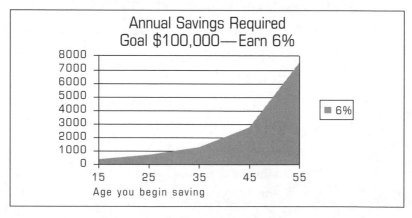

Annual Savings Required
Goal $100,000—Earn 6%

Even if you only begin saving $25 or $50 a month, you will be better off financially than if you do nothing! **MY ADVICE:** Don't delay —begin investing today.

9. TAKE ANY EMPLOYER MATCH IN YOUR COMPANY RETIREMENT PLAN

Social Security was never intended to provide for all your financial needs. For years it has been said that Social Security should be viewed as one leg of a three-leg stool. One leg is Social Security, the second leg is personal savings, and the third is your company pension plan. That's really a great concept.

A company-sponsored retirement plan can provide one of those legs. If you work for a company that offers a 401(k) plan or a 403(b) plan, sign up! A 401(k) plan is for "for-profit" companies, while a 403(b) plan is for "nonprofit" organizations.

These are called "pretax" plans. In other words, you don't have to pay tax on the money you put into the plan. You only have to pay taxes when you take money out of the plan.

I remember when I was on staff with Campus Crusade for Christ, I initially signed up for our 403(b) plan to invest $25 each month. Each year I would increase the amount.

Significantly, many employers offer to match all or a portion of your contribution. If your employer offers to match your portion, take it!

Some companies will match a specific dollar amount, or they will match up to a set percentage of your wages.

In other words, if you agree to invest $100, they will match it with a $100 investment. This is absolutely one of the best investment opportunities available. I know of no other investment that guarantees a 100 percent return on your investment on the first day!

If you do not take advantage of this offer, you are literally leaving money they are offering you on the table. It's like your boss came up to you and said, "Our company would like to give you $1,200 this year." But you simply smiled and said, "No thanks."

Now, I am assuming that your financial house is already in order, and you are not drowning in debt! If your house is not in order, you might consider putting it in order before committing a significant portion of your wages for your pension plan.

MY ADVICE: Take their money (and say thank you)!

10. INVEST IN IRAS

There are two kinds of investment retirement accounts, or IRAs, each with its distinct features for saving for your retirement.

TRADITIONAL IRA: PRETAX PLAN

You may qualify to invest in a traditional IRA. If you don't have a retirement plan at work, you can deduct your contributions on your taxes. (The tax deduction phases out if you participate in an employee-sponsored retirement plan and earn more than $50,000.) What does this mean? Well, if your income was $50,000 this year, but you invested $4,000 in an IRA, your taxable income would become $46,000 this year. However, you will be paying taxes when you begin to withdraw the money in retirement. In 2005 (if you qualify), the maximum annual contribution is $4,000 if you under age fifty, $4,500 if you are fifty or older.

Roth IRA: After-Tax Plan

You may qualify (based on adjusted gross income limits) to invest in a Roth IRA. The money you invest is money you have already paid taxes on. But, the great thing is that when you take the money out, you will not owe any taxes!

Like the traditional IRA, you and your spouse can each contribute up to $4,000 to a Roth IRA and an additional $500 if you are over age fifty. However, you must choose to contribute to either the traditional *or* Roth IRA, not both.

Be sure to check out specific IRS guidelines to be sure you qualify.

PERSONAL PREPARATION SUMMARY

Here is a list of my ten pointers to help you prepare financially for your retirement. Review them and then complete this chapter's Social Security Knowledge Quiz.

THE TEN PREPARATION POINTERS

❏ Establish written goals
❏ Use a MAP
❏ Save 10 percent, earn 8.5 percent
❏ Create an income-producing asset
❏ Engage in a steady investing program
❏ Begin retirement planning today
❏ Don't depend 100 percent on the federal government
❏ Take any employer match
❏ Become debt-free
❏ Invest in IRAs

NOTES

1. "Social Security Basic Facts"; www.ssa.gov/pressoffice/basicfact-alt.htm

2. www.whitehouse.gov/infocus/social-security/

3. "Social Security Basic Facts."

4. *Kiplinger's Personal Finance,* March 2005, 74.

5. Betsy Streisand, "Today's Retirement Journey," *U.S. News & World Report,* 14 June 2004, 47.

6. The book is available only through www.foundationsforliving.org

SOCIAL SECURITY KNOWLEDGE QUIZ

1. If a family earns an average of $23,000 per year, how much money will pass through their checking account during forty-five years?
   (a) $100,000 (c) $750,000
   (b) $500,000 (d) $1,000,000

2. What percent of their income will most families consume during their working life?
   (a) 10 percent (c) 70 percent
   (b) 50 percent (d) 100 percent

3. What percent of retirees say they wish they had saved more during their working life?
   (a) 10 percent (c) 50 percent
   (b) 20 percent (d) 70 percent

4. What is one of the first things you need to do when planning for retirement?
   (a) Sit down and establish goals.
   (b) Work harder.
   (c) Spend more.
   (d) Take a nap.

5. What will happen if you save 10 percent of your wages, earn 8.5 percent, and do this for forty-five years?
   (a) You will have an investment account equal to every penny your earned.
   (b) Nothing.
   (c) You will have $1 million.
   (d) Bill Gates will give you a phone call.

6. What should you do with an employer match for your retirement money?
   (a) Reject it.
   (b) Take it and say thank you.
   (c) Laugh at them.
   (d) Ignore the offer.

7. What is a key ingredient to your long term-financial plan?
   (a) Buy a new car every year.
   (b) Save 1 percent every year.
   (c) Pray Social Security benefits will go up.
   (d) Become 100 percent debt-free—including your mortgage.

8. What is the benefit of owning a rental property?
   (a) Your children can inherit it.
   (b) Its value should appreciate every year.
   (c) You can receive a check every month for the rest of your life.
   (d) All of the above

9. Who should be responsible to plan for your income needs during retirement?
   (a) Self
   (b) Government

10. Who should you primarily listen to for counsel?
    (a) *Money* magazine
    (b) Your spouse
    (c) Newspaper
    (d) Warren Buffett

CHAPTER 10

THE RETHINKING
OF RETIREMENT

Is it time we began
rethinking retirement?

AMERICANS HAVE BECOME OBSESSED
with the concept of retirement. They long for it, they
plan for it, and they can hardly wait for the day to arrive.
I have yet to understand why anyone forty-five years old
eagerly wants to become sixty-five years old.

There is one verse in the Bible that mentions retirement. It does not use the word *retirement,* but the concept
is communicated. In Numbers 8:25–26, God told Moses
the Levites were to be relieved from their work duties at
the age of fifty. "At the age of fifty they shall retire from
service in the work and not work any more." But those
retired priests and temple workers were still allowed to
assist their brothers.

This is an interesting thought to consider: Can
you imagine the apostle Paul planning for retirement?

How about the disciples? The word or concept was not even in their vocabulary!

Retirement as we know it today began back in 1935 when the Social Security Act designated the age of sixty-five for people to begin receiving retirement benefits. From that point on, everything began to change.

THE POSITIVE SIDE

There is definitely a positive aspect of retirement: more time. The question is, How are you going to use the forty-plus hours every week that you have been given? Think of all the wealth of knowledge and experience that could be shared with others. Think of all of the churches, mentoring groups, and ministries that would love to have your assistance (volunteer or paid).

Let me suggest four questions you can ask yourself:

- Is the purpose in life to work for forty to forty-five years and then simply retire?
- Am I "living" for retirement?
- How can I best use my talents to serve God today and after I am sixty-five?
- Why am I here on this earth?

My wife recently returned from a missions trip to Russia where she met a lady eighty-five years old. The woman had already traveled to 126 countries and was making plans to travel to at least twelve more in the next few years. Janet was so motivated by her life that she came home and said, "That's how I want to spend my life."

Great Models

I can think of several personal friends who made the decision to use their gifts and talents *even after they turned age sixty-five*. They are mentors, missionaries, teachers, church builders, consultants, pastors, neighborhood association leaders, church workers, volunteers, and even medical missionaries. They help those in need, spread kindness, visit hospitals and nursing homes, and generously give of their financial resources because they care about others and want to make a difference in this world.

They are ambassadors for Christ—every day.

Their eulogy will read, "I have fought the good fight, I have finished the course, I have kept the faith; in the future there is laid up for me the crown of righteousness, which the Lord, the righteous Judge, will award to me on that day; and not only to me, but also to all who have loved His appearing" (2 Timothy 4:7–8).

Their numbers are few, their hearts are big, and their rewards will be great. May God greatly increase their tribe!

Janet and I are far from being perfect, and we presently have to deal with few of the complications that come with age. At the writing of this book, we are both still in our late forties. Let me emphasize the late aspect! But two things have helped us to "stay on course" to this point and hopefully as we become older: (1) our goals, and (2) knowing whom we serve. We try to live every day as bond servants of Christ.

A Worthy Goal, a Worthy Master

You must have a purpose for your life, a goal that is so big it makes everything else that you want seem small.

You must have a goal that is worth any sacrifice, any hardship, or any suffering. You must have a goal that consumes your thoughts and motivates your soul. You must have a purpose so that when you look back at the end of your life, you will have no regrets. That goal will help you focus on the important things in life.

On the inside of our wedding bands, Janet and I have engraved our life verse: Romans 14:7–8. While we were engaged we memorized it, frequently talked about it, and made it an important part of our marriage. Here is what it says:

> For not one of us lives for himself, and not one dies for himself; for if we live, we live for the Lord, or if we die, we die for the Lord; therefore whether we live or die, we are the Lord's.

Life is too short and eternity too long not to be making the right decisions today.

Press on, my friend. *Finish strong!*

Answers to the
Social Security Knowledge Quizzes

Question	Ch.1	Ch.2	Ch.3	Ch.4	Ch.5	Ch.6	Ch.7	Ch.9
1	C	D	B	A	B	A	B	D
2	C	D	D	B	C	A	C	D
3	B	C	B	B	B	C	B	D
4	C	B	C	C	B	B	D	A
5	B	C	C	B	D	B	B	A
6	D	D	A	A	C	C	B	B
7	B	C	C	C	B	B	A	D
8	C	D	B	D	C	B	C	D
9	B	B	C	B	A	C	C	A
10	D	C	B	D	D	A	A	B

FINANCIAL ALERT UPDATES

How can I keep up-to-date on critical issues concerning Social Security?

New developments relating to Social Security are happening just about every day. On our Web site, www.foundationsforliving.org, I will keep you updated with developments as they unfold.

We are planning to offer the following on our Web site:

- Financial Alert Newsletter
- Important Web site links
- New developments
- New resources
- Updated articles from Ethan
- Additional documentation that was not published in this book

Go to www.foundationsforliving.org for the most updated information.

THE
SOCIAL SECURITY
TIME LINE

1929	The Great Depression arrives.
August 1935	President Franklin Roosevelt signs the Social Security Act, calling it "a law which will give some measure of protection to the average citizen and his family against the loss of a job and against poverty-ridden old age. . . . It will act as a protection to future Administrations against the necessity of going deeply into debt to furnish relief to the needy."
January 1937	First payroll taxes are paid. First one-time, lump-sum payment is made to Ernest Ackerman—a lump sum payment of seventeen cents. He had worked for one day (before retirement) under the Social Security program.
1939	Survivors' benefits and benefits for retirees spouses are added.

January 1940	Monthly benefits begin: Ida Mae Fuller receives the first official check in the amount of $22.54. She paid $24.75 in payroll taxes during her three years with the Social Security program, retired at age sixty-five, lived to be one hundred, and collected $22,888.92 in Social Security benefits.
1940	Five years after passage of the program, 222,488 people are receiving Social Security benefits.
1956	Disability benefits are added.
1960	The Supreme Court rules that individuals have no legal right to contributed dollars (Fleming v. Nestor).
1961	Act is amended to allow workers to receive reduced benefits beginning at age sixty-two.
1965	Congress establishes Medicare as health coverage to Social Security beneficiaries who are sixty-five and older. Sign up for program to begin on July 1, 1966.
1972	Congress adds automatic, annual cost-of-living allowances (COLAs), to begin in 1975.

1983	Congress saves Social Security—the SS system was only a few months away from checks not going out.
	President Reagan and Tip O'Neill (D) agree to (1) raise payroll taxes, (2) gradually increase retirement age to sixty-seven beginning in 2000, and (3) make Social Security benefits subject to income tax.
	Alan Greenspan gives leadership to the new program.
	The Social Security program is now in a position to pre-fund benefits.
January 1984	The president, vice president, federal judges, Congress, political appointees, and new federal government employees are covered under Social Security plan due to the 1983 Social Security reform act.
1996	The 1994–1996 Social Security Advisory Council propose three plans that each feature investing in financial markets.
March 1998	Senators Patrick Moynihan (D-NY) and Bob Kerry (D-Neb.) introduce legislation to allow optional personal accounts— private investments of up to 2 percent of wages.

| 1999 | SSA begins mailing annual statement to all workers ages twenty-five and older. Statements are mailed about three months before the worker's birthday. Prepared as an educational tool, the statement shows projected benefits. |

| 2001 | President's Commission to Strengthen Social Security meets, cochaired by Senator Moynihan and Robert Parsons, CEO of Time Warner. |

Almost seventy years after Social Security began, 47,688,000 receive payments. Of those sixty-five and older, 92 percent receive benefits.

| 2004 | Medicare begins deficit. |

Projections for 2008–2079 based on 2005 data.

| 2008 | More than 79 million baby boomers—those born between 1946 and 1964—are about to retire. Boomers born in 1946 turn age sixty-two (eligible for early retirement). |

| 2017 | Social Security will have to begin using interest received on treasury bonds, and later begin cashing in bonds (2027) in order to pay benefits. The fund will be depleted in 2041. SSA projects deficits will never end unless changes are made to program. |

2020	Spending for Medicare overtakes spending for Social Security in the early 2020s, and then soars off the chart.
2027	The Social Security Trust Fund will be $6.6 trillion, but will begin to decline in years to come. Interest on bonds will not make up the difference, and bonds will need to be cashed in.
2028	Baby-boomer retirement expenses begin to level off—twenty years after the boomer generation began to retire in 2008.
2041	Trust fund is 100 percent depleted. Payroll taxes are still flowing in, but they cover only about 74 percent of the benefits being paid out. Therefore, benefits need to be cut, age limit raised, taxes raised, or additional funding will be needed from the general budget.
2079	Projected benefits would be 68 percent without any changes.

SOCIAL SECURITY GLOSSARY

75-Year Actuarial Balance. The use of seventy-five years for projecting the future outlook is the typical form by which the SSA evaluates the program's long-term financial outlook.

Add-On. One aspect of private accounts that is being debated is, "Where is the money to fund private accounts going to come from?" The term "add-on" is used to imply the money will come from an addition payroll tax deduction. Currently a 12.4 percent payroll tax is being collected and deposited into the trust fund. Under a plan with private accounts, an additional 4 percent might be allowed to be deducted and directed toward your private account, for a total of 16.4 percent. (See "Carve-Out.")

Average Wage Index (AWI). This is the index used to help compute initial benefits for Social Security. It helps to convert a worker's past earnings to an equivalent value at age of retirement. Has been used for benefit calculations for workers retiring in 1979 and after.

Baby Boomers. Those born between 1946 and 1964 have been labeled "baby boomers," reflecting the large numbers born after World War II and during a period of relative prosperity in postwar America. An estimated seventy-nine million baby boomers will begin to retire in 2008.

Carve-Out. One aspect of private accounts that is being debated is, "Where is the money to fund private accounts going to come from?" The term "carve-out" is used to imply the money will come from current payroll tax deductions (unlike "Add-On" above, which would require an additional payroll tax deduction). Thus, assuming the current 12.4 percent payroll tax being collected and deposited into the trust fund, 4 percent might be directed toward your private account, and 8.4 percent would go directly to the Social Security Trust Fund.

Consumer Price Index (CPI). This is the official measure of inflation in consumer prices. The U.S. Department of Labor defines the consumer price index as "changes in the prices paid by urban consumers for a representative basket of goods and services."

Cost of Living Allowance (COLA). This is an annual increase in benefits to offset the effects of inflation. It is based on annual increases in consumer prices. The adjustments began to be automatic in 1975. Before that time they were occasional, whenever Congress decided to grant them.

Current Dollars. The amount given without any adjustment for inflation.

Debt-Free. Living 100 percent free of debt, including your mortgage.

Deficit. Each year when benefits being paid out (expenses) exceed payroll taxes (income), this creates a deficit.

Eligibility Age. Age when a person can begin to receive benefits. Those age sixty-two can begin to receive reduced benefits. Must be sixty-five to receive full benefits.

Employer Match. Some companies offer to match each dollar you invest in the company pension plan up to a specific dollar amount or percentage.

FICA (Federal Insurance Contributions Act). Taxes for Social Security benefits are collected under the authority of the Federal Insurance Contributions Act.

Government Accountability Office (GAO). The Government Accountability Office is the audit, evaluation, and investigative arm of Congress. It supports Congress in meeting its constitutional responsibilities and helps to improve the performance and accountability of the federal government for the American people. It provides Congress with professional, objective, fact-based, nonpartisan, and nonideological information when it is needed (www.gao.gov). Prior to 2004, the GAO was known as the General Accounting Office.

GDP (Gross Domestic Product). The gross domestic product represents the total value of goods and services produced in the United States.

Insured Worker. A fully insured worker has accumulated forty quarters of coverage. In 2005, $920 of taxable wages is required to obtain one quarter of coverage. The maximum number of quarters that can be earned in one year is four. Once you obtain forty quarters, you remain permanently insured.

Lockbox. A Social Security lockbox would ensure that the surplus Social Security Trust Fund money would not be spent each year by the federal government. Instead, the surplus money would remain under the control of the Social Security Administration.

MAP (Money Allocation Plan). A simple one-page per month budgeting system. Created by Ethan Pope in the 1980s.

Medicare. This is federal health insurance provided for those over sixty-five. It includes hospital and outpatient services and various forms of medical care. Began in 1965.

National Debt. The amount of debt owed by the United States of America.

New Deal. Beginning in 1933, Congress began passing numerous social and economic laws that had been proposed by President Franklin Roosevelt under what he called the "New Deal". New Deal programs enacted included the

Social Security Act, protection for labor unions, public works programs for employment, wage laws, social reform, benefits for unemployed, regulation for banks, creation of new jobs, and agricultural programs.

Normal Retirement Age. Age that a person can begin receiving Social Security benefits without a reduction in benefits.

OASDI. Old-Age, Survivors, and Disability Insurance.

Pay-As-You-Go. Money being paid in this year by workers will be used to pay out this year the retirement benefits of those already retired.

Payroll Taxes. Taxes paid out of workers' payroll checks into the Social Security program to fund Social Security benefits. Currently payroll taxes are 12.4 percent. The employee and employer each pay 6.2 percent for all wages up to $90,000 (2005).

Payroll Tax Revenue. Calculated by applying the payroll tax to taxable wages and self-employment income.

Ponzi Scheme. An illegal pyramid scheme named for Charles Ponzi. Operates on the "rob-Peter-to-pay-Paul" principle. Money coming in from new investors is used to pay older investors.

Progressive Indexing. Proposal to calculate Social Security benefits based on wage inflation for low-income workers and price inflation for high-income workers.

A sliding index would be used for middle-income workers. The use of progressive indexing would cause benefits for lower-income workers to grow faster than benefits for higher-income workers.

Privatize. To allow workers an opportunity to invest a portion of their Social Security payroll taxes into a private investment account.

Retirees. Those who are no longer working but are receiving Social Security benefits.

Surplus. Excess Social Security monies. Each year when payroll taxes (income) exceed benefits being paid out (expenses), this creates a surplus. (See "Social Security Trust Fund.")

SSA. Social Security Administration.

Social Security Act of 1935. Signed into law by President Franklin D. Roosevelt. In 2005 over forty-eight million Americans benefit from this legislation.

Social Security Trust Fund. Holds funds for excess Social Security money (surplus) that has been received but not yet spent. Very controversial because the federal government spends the surplus each year and gives the trust fund bonds that will be paid in the future.

Special Public Debt Obligations. Used exclusively by the Social Security Trust Fund. These special issue bonds cannot be bought or sold in the open market.

TSP (The Thrift Savings Plan). A voluntary retirement savings plan for federal employees, including members of Congress. These employees may participate in both TSP and Social Security.

Trust Funds. There are four trust funds in the Social Security Administration: (1) Social Security Old-Age and Survivor Insurance fund (OASI); (2) Disability Insurance fund (DI); together these first two funds are called OASDI; (3) Medicare Hospital Insurance fund (HI, or Medicare Part A for inpatient hospital and related care); and (4) the Supplemental Medical Insurance (SMI, or Medicare Part B for physician and outpatient services). Beginning in 2006, SMI will add Part D, a prescription drug benefit.

Trust Fund Short-Range Solvency Test. If the assets of the fund at the beginning of the year exceed 100 percent of the projected cost for that year, the trust fund is considered to have short-term adequacy (usually ten years).

Unemployment. Classification of someone who is seeking employment, but remains unemployed. The word *unemployment* was not even a word in English dictionaries before 1888.

Wage Cap Base: The maximum amount—the ceiling or cap—at which an employee's wages are subject to the Social Security payroll tax. Social Security taxes are deducted only for wages up to $90,000 (2005). (Medicare taxes have no cap.)

Worker: Those who are currently working and paying into the Social Security program.

APPENDIX A

SSA 2005 Annual Report Summary Facts and Projections[1]

2004 Benefits (p. 2)
48 million people received benefits
- 33 million retired workers and dependents
- 7 million survivors
- 8 million disabled and dependents

2004 Payroll Taxes (p. 2)
157 million people paid payroll taxes

2004 Trust Fund (in billions; p. 4)

Total Income	**$657.7**
• Taxes	$553.0
• Tax of benefits	15.7
• Interest	89.0
Total Expenses	**$501.6**
• Benefit payments	$493.3
• Railroad retire.	3.8
• Administrative exp.	4.5

Net Increase   **$156.1**

Balance at end of year   **$1,686.8**

Future of Trust Fund (p. 2)
2010–30   Rapid increase expected in expenses due to baby boomers retiring.

2017	Annual expenses will begin to exceed tax revenue.

2030   Expenses will continue to increase due to increase in life expectancy and low fertility rates, yet not as fast as previous twenty years.

2041   Trust fund assets will be exhausted.
Best case scenario: 2064
Worst Case scenario: 2032 (p. 161)

Unfunded Future Obligation—75 Years (p. 13)
2004 $3.7 trillion
2005 $4.0 trillion
The seventy-five-year unfunded obligation increased from $3.7 trillion (1/1/04) to $4 trillion (1/1/05). This represents a $300 billion increase in one year.

Unfunded Future Obligation—Infinite Horizon (p. 58)
2004 $10.4 trillion
2005 $11.1 trillion
The infinite horizon unfunded obligation increased from $10.4 trillion (1/1/04) to $11.1 trillion (1/1/05). This represents a $700 billion increase in one year (In present value).

Immediate Solutions to Solve for 75 Years (p. 3)
Raise payroll taxes 1.92 percent from 12.4 to
14.32 percent or
Reduce benefits 12.8 percent or
Add $4 trillion to trust fund balance from
federal budget

Immediate Solutions to Permanently Solve (p. 55)

Raise payroll taxes from 12.4 percent to
15.9 percent or
Reduce current and future benefits by 22 percent

Do-Nothing Solution (pp. 8, 16)

In 2041 immediately increase payroll tax to
16.66 percent and continue to increase to
18.10 percent in 2079 or
Immediately reduce benefits by 26 percent and
continue to do so until you reach
32 percent in 2079.

2041: Present tax rates would be able to pay
74 percent of scheduled benefits.

2079: Present tax rates would be able to pay
68 percent of scheduled benefits.

Projected Trust Fund Bond Interest Rates (p. 92)

Receiving 4.1 percent for 2003 bonds
Receiving 4.3 percent for 2004 bonds
Receiving 2.9 percent for last forty years

Trust Fund Bond Interest Rates for all bonds:
Range from 4.375 percent to 8.75 percent (p. 134)

1. Social Security Administration, "The 2005 Annual Report of the Board of Trustees of the Federal Old-Age & Survivors Insurance & Disability Insurance Trust Fund," 5 April 2005; www.ssa.gov/OACT/TR/TR05

NOTE: Pages in parentheses correspond to pages in annual report.

APPENDIX B

Tables and Charts

TABLE 1

Social Security
Trust Fund—Actual

(Selected Years—does not include Medicare)

Year	Total Receipts[1]	Total Expenditures	Net Increase/ Decrease[2]	Trust Fund Balance
	In millions	In millions	In millions	In millions
1937	767	1	766	766
1938	375	10	366	1,132
1939	607	14	592	1,724
1940	368	62	306	2,031
1945	1,420	304	1,116	7,121
	In billions	In billions	In billions	In billions
1950	2.9	1.0	1.9	13.7
1955	6.2	5.1	1.1	21.7
1956	6.7	5.8	.9	22.5
1957	8.1	7.6	.5	23.0
1958	9.1	8.9	.2	23.0
1959	9.5	10.8	-1.3	22.0
1960	12.4	11.8	.6	22.6
1961	12.9	13.4	-.5	22.2
1962	13.7	15.2	-1.5	20.7
1963	16.2	16.2	0.	20.7
1964	17.5	17.0	.5	21.2
1965	17.9	19.2	-1.3	19.8
1966	23.4	20.9	2.5	22.3
1967	26.4	22.5	3.9	26.3
1968	28.5	26.0	2.5	28.7

Year	Total Receipts[1]	Total Expenditures	Net Increase/ Decrease[2]	Trust Fund Balance
	In billions	In billions	In billions	In billions
1969	33.3	27.9	5.4	34.2
1970	37.0	33.1	3.9	38.1
1971	40.9	38.5	2.4	40.4
1972	45.6	43.3	2.3	42.8
1973	54.8	53.2	1.6	44.4
1974	62.1	60.6	1.5	45.9
1975	67.6	69.2	-1.5	44.3
1976	75.0	78.2	-3.2	41.1
1977	82.0	87.3	-5.3	35.9
1978	91.9	96.0	-4.1	31.7
1979	105.8	107.3	-1.5	30.3
1980	119.7	123.5	-3.8	26.5
1981	142.4	144.4	-2.0	24.5
1982	147.9	160.1	.2	24.8
1983	171.2	171.2	0	24.9
1984	186.6	180.4	6.2	31.1
1985	203.5	190.6	12.9	42.2
1986	216.8	201.5	4.7	46.9
1987	231.0	209.1	21.9	68.8
1988	263.5	222.5	41.0	109.8
1989	289.4	236.2	53.2	163.0
1990	315.4	253.1	62.3	225.3
1991	329.7	274.2	55.5	280.7
1992	342.6	291.9	50.7	331.5
1993	355.6	308.8	46.8	378.3
1994	381.1	323.0	58.1	436.4
1995	399.5	339.8	59.7	496.1
1996	424.5	353.6	70.9	567.0
1997	457.7	369.1	88.6	655.5
1998	489.2	382.3	106.9	762.5
1999	526.6	392.9	133.7	896.1

Year	Total Receipts[1]	Total Expenditures	Net Increase/ Decrease[2]	Trust Fund Balance
	In billions	In billions	In billions	In billions
2000	568.4	415.1	153.3	1,049.4
2001	602.0	439.9	163.1	1,212.5
2002	627.1	461.7	165.4	1,378.0
2003	631.9	479.1	152.8	1,530.8
2004	657.7	501.6	156.1	1,686.8

1. Includes interest income.

2. May not be exact due to rounding.

Source: From the charts "Trust Fund Data: Old-Age and Survivors Insurance Trust Fund, 1937–2004" and "Trust Fund Data: Old-Age, Survivors, and Disability Insurance Trust Funds, 1957–2004"; www.ssa.gov/OACT/STATS/table4a3.html; www.ssa.gov/OACT/STATS/ table 4a1.html

TABLE 1-P

Social Security Trust Fund—Projections

(Does not include Medicare Trust Fund)

Year	Total Receipts	Total Expenditures	Net Increase/ Decrease	Trust Fund Balance
	In billions[1]	In billions	In billions[2]	In billions
2005	689.9	526.6	163.3	1850.1
2010	922.5	682.4	240.1	2930.3
2015	1203.7	947.1	256.6	4211.1
2020	1524.2	1317.5	206.7	5378.5
2025	1855.5	1794.8	60.7	6012.6
2030	2195.0	2371.7	-176.7	5631.9
2035	2538.1	3026.1	-488.0	3836.0
2040	2881.6	3756.2	-874.6	272.7

1. Includes interest income.

2. May not be exact due to rounding.

Source: SSA 2005 Annual Report, 5 April 2005, 181.

Table 2

Percent of Social Security Benefits You Will Receive if You Retire at Different Ages

Birth Year	Year Turn 62	Normal Retire. Age (NRA)	Credit for each year of delayed retirement after NRA (percent)	Percent of Benefit Received If Retire at Age:				
				62	65	66	67	70
1924	1886	65	3	80	100	103	106	115
1925	1987	65	$3\,^1/_2$	80	100	$103\,^1/_2$	107	$117\,^1/_2$
1926	1988	65	$3\,^1/_2$	80	100	$103\,^1/_2$	107	$117\,^1/_2$
1927	1989	65	4	80	100	104	108	120
1928	1990	65	4	80	100	104	108	120
1929	1991	65	$4\,^1/_2$	80	100	$104\,^1/_2$	109	$122\,^1/_2$
1930	1992	65	$4\,^1/_2$	80	100	$104\,^1/_2$	109	$122\,^1/_2$
1931	1993	65	5	80	100	105	110	125
1932	1994	65	5	80	100	105	110	125
1933	1995	65	$5\,^1/_2$	80	100	$105\,^1/_2$	111	$127\,^1/_2$
1934	1996	65	$5\,^1/_2$	80	100	$105\,^1/_2$	111	$127\,^1/_2$
1935	1997	65	6	80	100	106	112	130
1936	1998	65	6	80	100	106	112	130
1937	1999	65	$6\,^1/_2$	80	100	$106\,^1/_2$	113	$132\,^1/_2$
1938	2000	65, 2 mo	$6\,^1/_2$	$79\,^1/_6$	$98\,^8/_9$	$105\,^5/_{12}$	$111\,^{11}/_{12}$	$131\,^5/_{12}$
1939	2001	65, 4 mo	7	$78\,^1/_3$	$97\,^7/_9$	$104\,^2/_3$	$111\,^2/_3$	$132\,^2/_3$
1940	2002	65, 6 mo	7	$77\,^1/_2$	$96\,^2/_3$	$103\,^1/_2$	$110\,^1/_2$	$131\,^1/_2$
1941	2003	65, 8 mo	$7\,^1/_2$	$76\,^2/_3$	$95\,^5/_9$	$102\,^1/_2$	110	$132\,^1/_2$
1942	2004	65, 10 mo	$7\,^1/_2$	$75\,^5/_6$	$94\,^4/_9$	$101\,^1/_2$	$108\,^3/_4$	$131\,^1/_4$
1943-1954	2005-2016	66	8	75	$93\,^1/_3$	100	108	132
1955	2017	66, 2 mo	8	$74\,^1/_6$	$92\,^2/_9$	$98\,^8/_9$	$106\,^2/_3$	$130\,^2/_3$
1956	2018	66, 4 mo	8	$73\,^1/_3$	$91\,^1/_9$	$97\,^7/_9$	$105\,^1/_3$	$129\,^1/_3$
1957	2019	66, 6 mo	8	$72\,^1/_2$	90	$96\,^2/_3$	104	128
1958	2020	66, 8 mo	8	$71\,^2/_3$	$88\,^8/_9$	$95\,^5/_9$	$102\,^2/_3$	$126\,^2/_3$
1959	2021	66, 10 mo	8	$70\,^5/_6$	$87\,^7/_9$	$94\,^4/_9$	$101\,^1/_3$	$125\,^1/_3$
1960 +	2022	67	8	70	$86\,^2/_3$	$93\,^1/_3$	100	124

Source: SSA 2005 Annual Report, p. 102.

TABLE 3

Social Security Beneficiaries (OASDI)
Receiving Monthly Benefits
(Does not include Medicare benefits)

Year	Beneficiaries	Year	Beneficiaries
1945	1,106,000	1990	39,471,000
1950	2,930,000	1995	43,107,000
1955	7,563,000	1999	44,366,000
1960	14,262,000	2004	47,367,000
1965	20,157,000	2025 P	76,406,000
1970	25,186,000	2045 P	93,284,284
1975	31,123,000	2065 P	103,189,000
1980	35,117,000	2080 P	110,640,000
1985	36,650,000		

Source: SSA 2005 Annual Report, p. 47.
P=Projected

TABLE 4

Social Security Payroll Tax
for Employee and Employer

Year of Tax Increase	Employer Tax	Employee Tax	Total Tax
1937	1.0	1.0	2.0
1950	1.5	1.5	3.0
1954	2.0	2.0	4.0
1957	2.25	2.25	4.50
1959	2.5	2.5	5.00
1960	3.0	3.0	6.0
1962	3.125	3.125	6.25
1963	3.625	3.625	7.25
1966	3.85	3.85	7.7
1967	3.9	3.9	7.8
1968	3.8	3.8	7.6
1969	4.2	4.2	8.4
1971	4.6	4.6	9.2
1973	4.85	4.85	9.7
1974	4.95	4.95	9.9
1978	5.05	5.05	10.1
1979	5.08	5.08	10.16
1981	5.35	5.35	10.7
1982	5.4	5.4	10.8
1984	5.7	5.7	11.4
1988	6.06	6.06	12.12
1990	6.2	6.2	12.4

Source: SSA 2005 Annual Report, p. 124.

APPENDIX C

Presidential Statement at the Signing of the Social Security Act

(AUGUST 14, 1935)

"Today a hope of many years' standing is in large part fulfilled. The civilization of the past hundred years, with its startling industrial changes, has tended more and more to make life insecure. Young people have come to wonder what would be their lot when they came to old age. The man with a job has wondered how long the job would last.

This social security measure gives at least some protection to thirty millions of our citizens who will reap direct benefits through unemployment compensation, through old-age pensions and through increased services for the protection of children and the prevention of ill health.

We can never insure one hundred percent of the population against one hundred percent of the hazards and vicissitudes of life, but we have tried to frame a law which will give some measure of protection to the average citizen and to his family against the loss of a job and against poverty-ridden old age.

This law, too, represents a cornerstone in a structure which is being built but is by no means complete. It is a structure intended to lessen the force of possible future depressions. It will act as a protection to future

Administrations against the necessity of going deeply into debt to furnish relief to the needy. The law will flatten out the peaks and valleys of deflation and of inflation. It is, in short, a law that will take care of human needs and at the same time provide the United States an economic structure of vastly greater soundness.

I congratulate all of you ladies and gentlemen, all of you in the Congress, in the executive departments, and all of you who come from private life, and I thank you for your splendid efforts in behalf of this sound, needed, and patriotic legislation.

If the Senate and the House of Representatives in this long and arduous session had done nothing more than pass this Bill, the session would be regarded as historic for all time."

FRANKLIN D. ROOSEVELT

Source: www.ssa.gov/history/fdrstmts.html#signing

ABOUT THE AUTHOR

ETHAN POPE is president of Foundations for Living, a ministry dedicated to helping people simplify and clarify life issues from a biblical and practical perspective. He is a graduate of Dallas Theological Seminary and a CERTIFIED FINANCIAL PLANNER™ professional, though he has never had a financial planning practice. Ethan is an author, speaker, and regular guest on national radio programs. His primary field of expertise is the theological and practical aspects of managing money.

Other books by Ethan Pope include *How to Be a Smart Money Manager, There's No Place Like Home, Creating Your Personal Money MAP, The Personal Finance Course,* and *Cashing It In.*

Ethan and his wife, Janet, have two adult children and live in Hattiesburg, Mississippi.

CONTACTING ETHAN POPE

FOR INFORMATION ON:

- Inviting Ethan Pope to speak in your city or church
- Ordering resources online
- Attending a Foundations for Living seminar in your area
- Receiving Foundations for Living publications

Visit our web site: **www.foundationsforliving.org**

Or write to: Ethan Pope, Foundations For Living,
P.O. Box 15356, Hattiesburg, MS 39404
(Phone) 601-582-2000

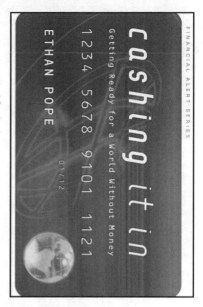

SINCE 1894, Moody Publishers has been dedicated to equip and motivate people to advance the cause of Christ by publishing evangelical Christian literature and other media for all ages, around the world. Because we are a ministry of the Moody Bible Institute of Chicago, a portion of the proceeds from the sale of this book go to train the next generation of Christian leaders.

If we may serve you in any way in your spiritual journey toward understanding Christ and the Christian life, please contact us at www.moodypublishers.com.

"All Scripture is God-breathed and is useful for teaching, rebuking, correcting and training in righteousness, so that the man of God may be thoroughly equipped for every good work."
— *2 TIMOTHY 3:16, 17*

MOODY
PUBLISHERS

THE NAME YOU CAN TRUST®

SOCIAL SECURITY TEAM

ACQUIRING EDITOR
Greg Thornton

COPY EDITOR
Jim Vincent

BACK COVER COPY
Laura Pokrzywa

COVER & INTERIOR DESIGN
The DesignWorks Group, Inc.
www.thedesignworksgroup.com

PRINTING AND BINDING
Versa Press, Inc.

The typeface for the text of this book is
StempelSchneidler